FIRST EDITION

MANAGING CONFLICT

AN INTROSPECTIVE JOURNEY TO NEGOTIATING SKILLS

Written and edited by Dorothy Balancio, Ph.D.

Mercy College

cognella®
academic publishing

Bassim Hamadeh, CEO and Publisher
Kassie Graves, Director of Acquisitions and Sales
Jamie Giganti, Senior Managing Editor
Miguel Macias, Senior Graphic Designer
John Remington, Senior Field Acquisitions Editor
Monika Dziamka, Project Editor
Trey Soto, Licensing Coordinator
Laureen Gleason, Production Editor
Joyce Lue, Interior Designer

Printed in the United States of America

ISBN: 978-1-5165-1724-4 (pbk) / 978-1-5165-1725-1 (br)

www.cognella.com   800-200-3908

CONTENTS

UNIT THREE 69

EMPATHY AND DEVELOPING NEGOTIATION SKILLS

UNIT FOUR 135

SOCIAL COMPETENCIES AND RESOLVING CONFLICTS

ACKNOWLEDGMENTS

Teaching managing conflict is one of the more important things that I do to contribute to our society. I believe that enabling the individual to reflect on himself or herself can produce wisdom (*self knowledge*) resulting in a way of understanding the world we live in. This book is constructed to be useful for those interested in improving their own relationships, as well as for those students interested in continuing their training to become professional negotiators and mediators.

I thank my Mercy students, colleagues, friends, and members of my family, from whom I have gained insight and understanding of the diversity of experience, perspective, and worldview. Every semester and every class in some important way is reflected in this work. They have simultaneously managed to keep me young and make me old.

Dr. Jeff Balancio and Dr. John Tucciarone have encouraged me and painstakingly reviewed, assessed, and edited my original manuscript. Their valuable feedback and faith in my work was supportive and enabled me to complete this book.

I conceived this book, but could not have done it on my own. I thank my contributors, all excellent teachers and researchers, committed to inspiring the next generation of critical thinkers and negotiators. I am indebted to: Sociologist Dr. Chelsea Kuo; Social Psychology Instructor Lindsay Astor; Education Professor Dr. Benita Bruster; Applied Sociologist Instructor Joey Palermo; Education Professor Dr. Ilene Rothschild; Education Professor Dr. Howard Miller; Political Scientist Professor Dr. Art Lerman; Psychology Instructor Nancy Friedman; International Relations Professor Michiko Kuroda; IMCR Trainer Dr. Stephen Slate; and Legal Studies Professors Diana and Paul Juettner.

Finally, I wish to acknowledge the spirit of my Louis, the wind beneath my wings. I love you, son.

PROLOGUE

HOW DO YOU DEVELOP MANAGING HUMAN CONFLICT SKILLS?

The more I study and teach sociology, the more I love the subject. No other area of intellectual work overlaps with so many other fields of knowledge; none connects the sciences and the humanities so directly or offers such a variety of insights into our current world. Sociology is distinctive in the attention it pays to what lies *between* people, to what *links* individuals with others in the social world. We are people watchers. There is a commitment to use observations of the real world over time to develop explanations that are even better than the ones we already have.

This book presents a sociological perspective of cooperation, conflict, and conflict resolution. The main mission is to invite the reader to think beyond individuals in isolation and focus on negotiation skills that are competencies for building connected trusting relationships and good communication. The aim is to broaden students' horizons, improve their emotional intelligence, sharpen their observational skills, and strengthen their analytical capabilities. The focus is on trust, self-worth, values, goals, moral code (whether we are active producers or passive receivers of our moral code), roles, statuses, and healthy relationships.

The field of conflict studies is a mutt. There are parts borrowed from sociology, psychology, political science, philosophy, social psychology, communication, law, anthropology, education, counseling, human relations, business, administration, economics, history, labor relations, international relations, and community health.

My students and colleagues at Mercy College encouraged the writing of this text. Some students are younger traditional undergraduates, while others are older adults going back to school after many years in the real world. All wanted clear information about the social analysis of human behavior in conflict, including awareness of self, self-motivation, values, goals, and self-regulation, with a focus on trust, moral code, and moral judgment. Most were interested in how to handle relationships, specifically with an emphasis on empathy and the social skills. Students also pointed out that they wanted the theories and research to have real-world application. This book applies abstract concepts to exercises and activities in concrete ways related to their particular interests and concerns. Throughout this text, an effort is made to strike a balance between theory and practice. Most of the discussions, concepts, activities, and illustrations are based on American culture and the social changes that have occurred and are occurring in the United States today.

This book is an introspective journey of self-awareness, self-motivation, self-regulation, empathy, and social competencies. The emphasis is to help the reader to understand the self, whom to trust, how to understand others, and how to negotiate in order to have successful trusting relationships. My thesis is based on the belief that understanding whom we can really trust is critical in life because evil exists. True wisdom is self-knowledge.

GENESIS

HOW DID THIS PROJECT EVOLVE?

This is the genesis of this work and the evolving program at Mercy College.[1] For over two decades, I have been actively engaged with two brilliant, compassionate colleagues (now close friends) from different disciplines (legal studies and political science). We make up a very successful team (team teaching and collaborative learning).[2] My team partners are Diana Juettner and Art Lerman. We are the three musketeers of the academy.[3]

I am a sociologist who has studied urban communities, family, gender roles, and stratification, and brings instrumental breadth and depth to our academic collaborative team through my M.A. and Ph.D. in sociology, master's of philosophy, master's of pedagogy, and several postdoctoral certifications (including IMCR Mediator, Family Life Course Education, N.Y.S. Teacher, Career Management, and Decision Making). I was a senior trainer with consulting experience in many private and public environments. I provided career and outplacement counseling in individual as well as group formats in addition to developing and teaching a wide variety of behavioral science courses.

Professor Diana Juettner, attorney, brings the experiences of a legal studies program director, a practicing lawyer, an elected official, and a volunteer mediator and arbitrator. Like her colleagues, she was heavily involved in campus governance and in the teaching of broad-based undergraduate legal studies and conflict studies curriculums.

Professor Arthur Lerman, political scientist, began studying the literature in communication, conflict management, and democracy in the 1960s. His dissertation (Ph.D. Princeton University) on research on legislatures; fieldwork in Taiwan; and involvement in his own academic, ethnic, and civic society, including involvement in campus governance, provided his work with a strong multicultural, comparative, and hands-on component. All this was grounded in many years of teaching a broad-based undergraduate curriculum (e.g., world history and comparative politics) to a multicultural (ethnic, religious, social class) student population. He was named Mediator of the Year and is a coordinator of the IMCR/Mercy Community Mediation Center.

NOTES

1. Currently, there are fourteen undergraduate sections of four courses and two graduate courses. Every January there is mediation training for those interested in community mediation (IMCR's thirty-five-hour NYS certified training)—on average, 700 students. There are fourteen faculty members teaching in classrooms and online.

2. We published and presented "Can Professors Learn in the Classroom? Team Teaching Conflict Management Skills" at the International Conference on Social Values in Oxford University, England. (2002).

3. Together we have more than 100 years of teaching experience.

MISSION

WHAT ARE DISTINCTIVE FEATURES OF THIS TEXT?

The main mission of this book is to have the reader take an introspective journey that will facilitate the development of negotiation skills in resolving conflicts. There should be an understanding of social relationships and communication. The aim is to broaden students' horizons, improve their emotional intelligence, sharpen their observational skills, and strengthen their analytical capabilities. I focus on self-awareness, self-regulation (connection with one's moral code), self-motivation, empathy, and negotiation skills. This journey includes a discovery of attitudes, values, and goals that enable individuals to internalize norms (rules that govern behavior). As a result, readers should examine their reflexive self and social mirrors.

Hopefully, it becomes clear that becoming an active producer of one's moral code will facilitate the development of trusting relationships. Developing trusting relationships is one measure of a successful negotiation. Ideally, success can be measured if one can inspire trust in a suspicious opponent. Negotiation is an art that depends upon the specific competencies that are addressed in this book.

The study of conflict resolution, negotiation, and mediation attracts a diverse student population. The reader will explore whether these theories are useful in the resolution of conflict. Theoretical paradigms, strategies, techniques, and illustrations of conflict resolution are introduced to the beginning student with a focus on developing negotiation skills. The book's objectives are to have the reader gain factual knowledge (terminology, classifications, methods) and learn fundamental principles, generalizations, and theories.

Another objective is the application of learning; that is, to improve critical thinking, problem-solving, and decision-making. This book can be used alone, in conjunction with other texts, or as a supplement to a comprehensive series of classroom lectures and discussions about conflict resolution. This work may be viewed as a geological investigation of the shifting ground upon which we stand in our contemporary relationships. Beginning the journey with introspection seems to be the wise approach.

> If there is right in the soul, there will be beauty in the person. If there is beauty in the person, there will be harmony in the home. If there is harmony in the home, there will be peace on earth.
>
> —Chinese proverb

Additionally, the reason this book suggests many practice exercises and activities is to encourage deeper learning of the material discussed.

> Tell me and I forget. Teach me and I remember. Involve me and I learn.
>
> —Ben Franklin, who took it from a Chinese proverb

The text's specific learning outcomes: the reader will become familiar with the language of conflict management and how disputes are handled through *preparation, critical thinking,* and *introspection*; the reader will identify the constructive and destructive environments of conflict; and the reader will be introduced to strategies and techniques successfully used in dispute resolution.

UNIT ONE

INTRODUCTION

CHAPTER 1

WHAT IS CONFLICT STUDIES AND HOW DOES IT FIT INTO THE LARGER ACADEMIC DISCIPLINES?

In all cultures there are traditions of dispute resolution, violent and nonviolent. People generally have a negative connotation of conflict. However, conflict can be managed and can build relationships. When you think it through, conflict is a prerequisite to creativity. Conflict keeps relationships interesting and can motivate change. The resolution of conflict can address serious long-term problems. Conflict does not have to be destructive. We can establish a constructive environment for the conflict. Conflict is related to the opportunity to strengthen one's understanding, but not without risk or danger. There are costly consequences of conflict. Therefore, this book is designed to use conflict creatively by taking the reader on a journey from self-awareness to successfully connecting in trusting relationships. It is important to keep in mind that conflict is inevitable; there is no life without conflict. Actually one might make a case that the foundation of our civilization rests on conflict.

It is argued by scholars that this field has now developed its own literature and academic programs and should therefore be considered a discipline. Other scholars argue that most of the work is produced by people who are identified with more established disciplines of sociology, history, law, and political studies. Actually, there is a full range of social sciences, humanities, mathematics, and biology that study conflict. The professionals in this field are academics, practitioners, mediators, arbitrators, trainers, lawyers, ombudsmen, counselors, consultants, HR professionals, teachers, administrators, ministers, social workers, security specialists, labor relations negotiators, and law enforcement personnel. Broadly speaking there are basic issues in the field centering on the nature of conflict, the most valued elements in conflict, and the best way to handle conflict. Conflicts within the the field are discipline versus non-discipline, ideological and value conflicts, theoretical versus applied, universal versus relativists, and grandiose versus picayune.

This text recognizes several approaches and uses them in presenting the skills-oriented approach with diverse material to enhance and clarify. This diverse material focuses on:

- a sociological/social psychological approach (know the parties; that is, self and others), understand the individual's role in communication and relationships
- a pluralistic approach to defining issues (along with creating a menu of options)
- a combination of theoretical approaches (when possible, focusing on self and others' interests), understand the legitimacy/history approach (brainstorm options and relate to history)
- a focused approach on establishing the trusting connected relationships reflected in the agreement(s), understand the exit strategy

Because much of this book pivots on a journey of introspection, individuals can better understand their own actions and their interpretation of the reactions of other people. By understanding self, we can understand how we view the world because we do not see people as they are, but we see them as we are. We see them through our lenses (our culture). We first define then we see. This text incorporates a symbolic interactionist perspective.

There are several important theorists who inspired me and are reflected in the pages of this text. Two thinkers who established the environment and practical aspects of the field for me are Morton Deutsch and Roger Fisher. They were the hook that drew me into the academic discipline.

Professor and social theorist Morton Deutsch, a respected voice in the field, explains why he became obsessed with conflict resolution:

> Throughout my career in social psychology, I have been concerned with the interrelations among experimental research, theory, and social policy. I started my graduate study not long after Hiroshima and Nagasaki, and my work in social psychology has been shadowed by the atomic cloud ever since.[1]

Deutsch made a major contribution to conflict theory and to the practical problems of conflict resolution. Deutsch[2] adds to the definition by stating, "Conflict exists whenever incompatible activities occur [...]. An action which is incompatible with another action prevents, obstructs, interferes with, injures or in some way makes it less likely or less effective." Deutsch also distinguishes five types of conflict: intrapersonal (within the self), interpersonal (between individuals), intragroup (within a group), intergroup (between groups), and international (between nations). I particularly want to focus on his work on destructive and constructive environments for conflict. He addresses factors that relate to whether a conflict is constructive (that is, satisfied) or destructive (that is, unsatisfied). A conflict that is satisfied/constructive results in innovation, understanding, creative solutions, willingness to move (that is, be flexible), constructive change, sense of growth, enhanced relationship; that develops trust, restores respect to the parties, and clarifies values. A conflict that is unsatisfied/destructive results in anger that lingers after the conflict, affects other aspects of the relationship, alters the system, increases distrust, does not restore respect to the parties; that adds physical stress, violence, and negative self-worth/self-esteem; and shuts things down in hostility.[3] His work reflects his concerns with the interrelations among experimental research, theory, and social policy. His efforts contributed to the understanding of how to prevent destructive conflict and initiate cooperation. Deutsch can be connected with symbolic interactionism, which will be discussed in the later chapters of this text.

Roger Fisher's less theoretical and more practical work came out of Harvard University; he presents step-by-step procedures for effective conflict intervention and conflict management. He was the director of the Harvard Negotiating Project and was a leading source of inspiration for different types of theory and practice in negotiation. Fisher, like Deutsch, was motivated to dedicate his career to the field. The bombing of Pearl Harbor happened while he was studying at Harvard. He joined the U.S. Army Air Force along with his classmates. After the war he returned to the university to continue his studies, faced with the reality that many of his classmates had been killed. He vowed to spend the rest of his life working to ensure that a war like World War II never happened again.

Professor Fisher and his colleagues[4] offer powerful advice for dealing with tough negotiations. Their work presents a step-by-step, powerful approach to prepare for a successful negotiation. The basic elements of negotiation are relationship, communication, interests, options, legitimacy, BATNA (Best Alternative to a Negotiated Agreement), and commitments (see 1.1 APPLIED EXERCISE). The principles, insights, and wisdom found in *Getting to Yes: Negotiating Agreement without Giving In*[5] and *Getting Together: Building Relationships as We Negotiate*[6] have inspired our work with our students. Their books include many practical guidelines on how to focus on the merits of issues, and not on position bargaining. That is, going behind the position to the underlying interests of the parties.

Fisher and his co-author William Ury highlight several main points when giving their advice on successful principled negotiation:

First: separate the people from their positions. Focus on the problem and keep in mind that you, and the other party, have important needs and concerns.

Second: focus on interests, not positions. Try to uncover the interests that are behind the position. Focus the discussion on how your interests and those of the other party can be met.

Third: be sure that all options have been considered. Encourage brainstorming for options in order to add to the understanding of the range of possibilities.

Fourth: strive for fairness by framing the agreement with objective criteria and general principles. Both sides should recognize the proposed principles as fair and therefore feel the resulting agreement is fair.

However, we understand that there are problems with their advice if it is taken as a universal model for every negotiation because it may not always be possible to find central principles that everyone can agree with. Also, the parties may view the criteria differently and sometimes position bargaining is a traditional part of formal negotiations. These points will be discussed in Unit IV of this text.

One of the core purposes of this introductory, skills-based book is to guide the reader on an introspective journey to acquire the personal and social competencies necessary to negotiate successfully.

There has definitely been a dialogue through the centuries. It is important to understand not only the practical, but also the social philosophers and theorists who have studied the question of conflict and the resolution of conflict.

WHY ARE THEORETICAL PARADIGMS USEFUL?

Many students ask, Why study theory? I frequently answer with the following example: imagine you are looking at a full moon with all its shadows, craters, impressions, elevations clearly visible on a cloudless night. It would be difficult to have an in-depth conversation

Fig. 1.1 Moon

Copyright © Gregory H. Revera (CC BY-SA 3.0) at https://commons.wikimedia.org/wiki/File:FullMoon2010.jpg.

about specific points on the moon's surface. However, if you take a picture of the moon and superimpose a premeasured grid system on the image, everyone in the discussion could focus on very specific features being described by using coordinates to pinpoint the location you want to discuss.

Theory is like a grid placed on a photograph of the observed reality. It does not appear when you look up at the moon, but it helps you to discuss and analyze the surface features of the moon. The moon represents the real world, and the artificial, imposed grid system is the theory. Now, with the ordered, numbered grid, it is easier to discuss and analyze those interest points on the moon's surface. For example, look at C4 or E7. We all are focused on the same points. Theory helps us to analyze reality and share that insight with others.

I would add that there really is no practice without theory. Theory is just the explanation for what you are doing. You may be so used to doing certain things that you forgot why—or the why has never been clearly articulated in your mind and it remains implicit. But even so, what you are doing is based on an explanation. A simple illustration: pour water into a glass. There is a theory of physics that explains what you are doing. If you forget the proper practice and just pour the water near the glass, you will quickly be reminded of the theory (explanation) of why you have to aim more carefully.

1.1 APPLIED EXERCISE: NEGOTIATION PREPARATION[7]

This is successfully used as a frame for preparing to negotiate. This model can be used for effective negotiation planning: apply the model and use it in practice.

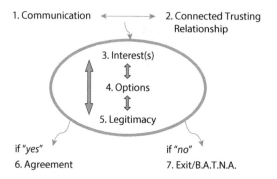

Fig. 1.2 The Seven Elements

Table 1.1: The Seven Elements

(BEST ALTERNATIVE TO A NEGOTIATED AGREEMENT, YOUR EXIT/WALK-AWAY)

1.	2.	3.	4.	5.	6.	7.
Relationship	Communication	Interest	Options	Legitimacy	Agreement	Alternative
parties' current and preferred relationship	plan meeting: -purpose -people -process	list needs and concerns	list options	identify laws, codes, standards, and procedures	elements of an agreement	BATNA* exit walk-away
plan dialogue	gap	list hopes and fears	for each issue	relevant to options	our and their authority	WATNA** exit walk-away
steps to *changes* that lead to the preferred relationship	listen and identify different conversations intent/impact *changes*	theirs and ours separate people from position	brain-storming	relevant to issues	commitment: when? what level? -thoughts -tentative -firm -sign deal	ours and theirs

*BATNA: best alternative to a negotiated agreement
**WATNA: worst alternative to a negotiated agreement

There are different emphases in every topic: theory oriented (analytical) emphasis, and applied or pragmatic (what works in a specific situation) emphasis. Both are a must and both are presented. The seven elements are practical and are useful in preparing for a negotiation.

1.2 APPLIED EXERCISE: FIRST NEGOTIATION AS A GROUP IN CLASS

Establish a contract with your students by negotiating the set of rules and ethics—establish the classroom conduct for the semester.

You don't use the same set of rules for basketball that you use for football or baseball. It is the same with all parts of your life. The rules of the college are different from the rules outside the institution. The rules of this class are specific to facilitating the basic sociology learning objectives.

SUMMARY OF LEARNING OUTCOMES AS SPECIFIED IN THE SYLLABUS

At the conclusion of this course the student should have a basic understanding of conflict and the techniques to establish cooperation. The student should be familiar with relevant theoretical paradigms and the various strategies, techniques, and approaches of resolving conflict.

I,_____, read, understand, and will abide by the requirements outlined in the syllabus. Additionally, I will comply with the agreed-upon rules and ethics of our class as outlined below:

_____
_____
_____
_____
_____
_____
_____
_____
_____
_____
_____
_____
_____
_____
_____
_____
_____
_____
_____

Signature: Student signs_____Date: _____

Signature: Faculty Member signs __Date: _____

1.3 APPLIED EXERCISE: GROUP NEGOTIATION FROM DYADS (TWO-MEMBER GROUPS) TO NEGOTIATING WITH THE ENTIRE CLASS[8]

Negotiating a trip: begin with each person choosing a place that they would like to visit for an all-expenses-paid vacation sponsored by the college. Travel, food, and lodgings will be paid for, but only if agreement on one destination can be negotiated unanimously.

After everyone has chosen a place, team him or her up with someone who has selected a different place. Then, the two must negotiate to come up with one destination. The dyads then put together with another pair (going to a different place) and the four must negotiate to go to a single destination. When the four agree, they are put with another four who are heading somewhere else. The groups of eight negotiate until they reach an agreement. Then, the group of sixteen negotiates to choose the final destination.

Remind the class that they need to have unanimous agreement for the single destination.[9]

Debrief

- Describe how you felt negotiating with one person.
- Describe how you felt when two of you had to negotiate together with another dyad.
- Did you prefer negotiating in small or larger groups? Explain.
- Describe how you felt about the final negotiation.
- Who stood out? Why?
- What did you like about the experience?
- What did you dislike about the experience?
- How does this connect to our examination of listening and communicating?

NOTES

1. Deutsch, M. (1973). *The Resolution of Conflict: Constructive and Destructive Processes.* New Haven and London: Yale University Press. ix.

2. 1971a, p. 51/Deutsch, M. "Toward an Understanding of Conflict." *International Journal of Group Tensions,* I, 42–54, 1971a.

3. For a more detailed discussion, see Deutsch's *The Resolution of Conflict: Constructive and Destructive Processes* (1973). New Haven and London: Yale University Press, in which he presents his six conflict typologies: contingent conflict, displaced conflict, vertical conflict, misattributed conflict, latent conflict, and false conflict.

4. William Ury, Bruce Patton, Scott Brown, and Daniel Shapiro are some of those who worked with Roger Fisher at Harvard University on workshops and books. My colleagues and I attended the Program of Instruction for Lawyers (PIL) at Harvard: "Negotiation," "Advanced Negotiation," and "Mediation" workshops.

5. Roger Fisher, William Ury, and Bruce Patton. *Getting to Yes.* (1988). United States: Houghton Mifflin Company.

6. Roger Fisher and Scott Brown. (1989). *Getting Together: Building Relationships as We Negotiate.* New York: Penguin Books.

7. Model derived from the practical advice of Roger Fisher and William Ury.

8. This exercise was part of Dr. Steven Slate's IMCR mediation training.

9. I have been doing this activity for years with IMCR Director Dr. Steven Slate and with Mercy students—there was never a group that could come to an agreement. The group admitted they would rather give up a free trip than to give in to a classmate.

CHAPTER 2

AN OVERVIEW

Many of us have been programmed by our upbringing to think conflict is a bad thing, something to be avoided, but recent scholarship and professional practice have argued the opposite. Conflict, handled in a nonviolent way, can be positive, even crucial for improving social relationships at both interpersonal and overarching social structural levels of society.

So let's look at conflict from a historical perspective: one can argue that the foundations of our civilization(s) rest on conflict. The Western tradition, after all, begins with two great books of conflict: Homer's *The Iliad* (for example, Achilles/Agamemnon, Greeks/Trojans) and the Bible (at least, Moses/Pharaoh, Jacob/Esau). Chinese civilization is said to have begun with a great battle won under the leadership of the Yellow Emperor (2698–2598 BC) and Indian civilization looks back to the God Indra slaying "the firstborn of dragons." Yet, even in these earlier times, conflict had its positive handling. *The Iliad* is much about how Achilles, hero of the Greeks, and Priam, King of the Trojans, weep together over the losses of war and agree to a generous truce in their conflict. The Bible presents dramatic scenes of the reconciliations of Isaac and Ishmael and of Jacob and Esau. Chinese history turns into a quest for peace as its poets write, "One general, merit achieved, ten thousand bones dry." And the Indian emperor Ashoka (269 BC) is famous for renouncing war and dedicating himself to the welfare of his people. Throughout history, civilization's sages have continued to search for ways to use conflict for the better. Aristotle, for example, warned the victorious in political conflicts to maintain magnanimity, to never push their advantage so far as to drive the defeated to desperation and rebellion. Or, going even further, Rabbi Nathan's, "Who is strong? He who can turn an enemy into a friend."

As modern students of conflict, let us follow proper social science practice and stop to define our terms. What, after all, is this conflict we are writing about? Because there are several definitions of the term *conflict*, I want to begin with an American sociologist because his definition clearly frames the material of this text. Coser[1] introduced the conflict perspective into American sociology with his definition of "a struggle over values and claims to scarce status, power, and resources in which the aims of the opponents are to neutralize, injure, or eliminate their rivals." Or another way of stating this, an individual or group striving for a goal and finding obstacles raised by others standing in the way.

Recent social science has doubled down on these themes, specifically by seeking the scientific method to refine and develop these reflections on conflict coming to us throughout history. Though we should not forget that Aristotle used inductive logic and the comparative method on the best empirical evidence he could muster. It could be argued that Aristotle was already pretty much up to modern social science standards. James A. Schellenberg's text, *Conflict Resolution: Theory, Research, and Practice* (1996), categorized conflict from three perspectives: the nature of individual psychology (intrapersonal perspective), interpersonal relations (microscopic symbolic interactionism perspective), and overarching structure of society (macroscopic perspective).

The modern intrapersonal perspective is usually seen as beginning with Sigmund Freud with his characterization of the basis of all human psychology of the instincts for destruction and for love. When the two intermingle in each person's psychology, the instinct for destruction often has greater force than the instinct for love. Theorists such as Herbert Spencer and Konrad Lorenz continued Freud's pessimism. They painted the human psychology, at its base, as deeply aggressive and dangerous. Additional thinking and research on these themes came up with human nature as being cooperative. This can be traced back to the social contract theorist Jean-Jacques Rousseau (1712–1778), who felt the state of nature was an ideal one and this explains his social philosophy. In his early essays[2] the central idea was that "Man is naturally good, and only by institutions is he made bad." Another trend that related to these themes was that no matter what the most basic nature is, it is so influenced by *social learning*. This view stated that a person's basic nature, in itself, is rather unimportant. Sociologists and social psychologists focus on how the social conditions influence our lives as individuals. *Social conditions* are the realities of the life that we create together as social beings, the aspects of society that emerge out of human interaction.

Besides the microscopic interactionist paradigm, the fundamental theoretical paradigms of macroscopic conflict theory and macroscopic functionalism are used throughout this book. To clarify terms, the microscopic perspective has also included individual characteristics theories, interpersonal theories, and small group theories. The macroscopic perspective has been labeled theories of the social structure.[3] Some of the key theorists who dealt with the important questions about what links the individual and society are Marx, Simmel, Smith, Merton, Mead, Cooley, James, Dewey, Blumer, Freud, and Darwin.

Macroscopic conflict theory examines how power affects the distribution of scarce resources and how conflict changes society. Conflict theory holds that power is just as important as shared values in holding society together. Conflict is responsible for social change. For Karl Marx (1818–1883), the father of conflict theory, the individual's interests must be subordinated to those interests of the collective. Marxism is based on the belief that there are divisions in society that drive different interests. These different interests are imbedded in laws (the formal, written, institutionalized norms). This radical macroscopic perspective seeks radical changes in society. Marx, reflecting the dialectic philosophy that preceded him, developed a political and economic analysis based on assumptions that conflict is an inevitable part of society. Marxists encourage conflict, unlike Adam Smith, who wanted to live in peace. Marx, in his dialectic materialism, determined that conflict promotes further conflict; that change is inevitable; and that, in his opinion, this change moves in the direction of an improved human condition.

Prior to Marx, Adam Smith (economist and theorist of the late 18th century) espoused that the market balanced the self-interests of individuals continually. On one side of the market was supply of goods or services; that is, how much was available. On the other side was demand or how much people wanted. Smith is better defined as a conflict resolution theorist than a conflict theorist. Smith developed the invisible hand theory.

German sociologist Georg Simmel (1858–1918) argued that conflict is necessary as a basis for the formation of alliances. According to Simmel (also interested in the role of conflict in social change), conflict is one means whereby a web of group affiliations is constructed. The continual shifting of alliances within the web of social groups can help explain who becomes involved in social movements and how much power those movements are able to acquire. Conflict theorists point out that the role of power is just as important as the influence of shared beliefs in explaining why society does not disintegrate into violent chaos. For them, important questions are who benefits from the exercise of power and who loses. These questions are central to conflict theory.

German scholar Max Weber (1864–1920) made important contributions to sociological thought and was influential in the areas of stratification, bureaucracy, and religion. He opposed some aspects of Marxian theory, believing that changing values, rather than conflict, are a major source of social change. Weber introduced status and power to Marx's economic classes. He defined power as "the probability that one actor within a social relationship will be in a position to carry out his own will despite resistance."[4] Weber's wide-ranging research used examples from the history of societies all over the world.

German social theorist Rolf Dahrendorf (1959) departed from the Marxian view that the conflicting economic classes of the exploiters and the exploited would bring about social change. Dahrendorf finds conflict among many kinds of groups and in every institution. Any power differentiation (for example, student/professor, mother/child) within and between groups provides a basis for conflict. This conflict produces social change at all times, but the change is not always revolutionary. We cannot change our laws, our bureaucracies, or even our families, for example, without first experiencing conflicts among various group and individual interests.

Macroscopic functionalism examines how society is structured and how social structures work together as a system to perform the major functions of society. Functionalists (a view that relates to the unitary perspective) believe in togetherness, oneness, and connectedness. Systems that are healthy are adaptive, can maintain patterns of the system, are integrative, and can attain system goals. Functionalists believe conflict is harmful to the system and that this harm is brought about by deviance. They believe the objective is system maintenance. Putting it in a positive way, functionalism is showing what has to be fixed. European Emile Durkheim's (1859–1917) work led to an emphasis on the study of social structures and their functioning. American functionalists Talcott Parsons (Harvard University) and Robert Merton (Columbia University) were strongly influenced by Durkheim. From the functionalist perspective, society holds together because its members share the same basic beliefs about how people should behave. Functionalism asks how societies carry out the functions they must perform.[5]

Microscopic *symbolic interactionism* examines how:

- people behave in intimate groups
- symbols and communication shape perception
- social roles are learned and society is constructed through interaction

The basic perspective of Adam Smith can be described as interactionist. These thinkers focused primarily on how social structures are created in the course of human interaction; that is, the interpersonal relationship (including conflict).

William Isaac Thomas used what we would now describe as a social-psychological framework for examining the behavior of the people studied.[6] Thomas's colleague George Herbert Mead (1863–1931) was concerned with linking the individual with society, which is in finding out how people construct a sense of self that incorporates the teachings of society. Mead thought of the self as emerging out of social interaction. People develop distinct personalities from the way in which they have been taught to play the roles they are given. This instruction of roles takes place at the micro level of interaction among small groups of people (for example, family and friendship groups). This is accomplished through language and nonverbal communication. He explains that we "first define the world then see it; we 'see' things as we are, not as they are. Therefore, in order to have 'meaning,' it is critical to know the self and to know the other." Actually, this follows Adam Smith's theory of moral sentiments and can also be connected with Mead.

Charles Horton Cooley, like Mead, believed strongly that the self is a social product. We acquire a self by observing and assimilating the identities of others. Cooley's looking-glass self is the reflection of our self that we think we see in the behavior of others toward us. He says we are always looking for behavior cues of others, wondering what they think about us. William James and John Dewey also contributed to this approach that came to be identified in 1937 by Herbert Blumer (student of Mead) as symbolic interactionism. In short, this perspective emphasizes that behavior can be fully understood only if we take into account its reflexive character, and that the meaning we apply grows first and foremost out of interaction.[7]

Another theoretical giant who influenced our work is Sigmund Freud. Freud, the creator of modern psychoanalysis, was the first social scientist to develop a theory of personality and child development that specified how society's norms are incorporated into the self. Freud's theory leans heavily on the effects of conflict among family members. He studied personality and described the parts of the individual as struggling. Freud believed there was internal conflict, which is an internal combat of various psychodynamic forces for control over the ego. One could see that this reflects Plato's theory of self.

The symbolic interactionists were influenced by the work of Freud and their theories were trying to correct his theory of internal conflict, that is, intrapersonal conflict. Interactionists see conflict as interpersonal.

Charles Darwin was also interested in the struggle within species for survival of the fittest. For Darwinists, the productive outcome of the conflict was the survival of the individuals who have a genetic anomaly that is most adaptive to the environment and therefore will pass these genes to their offspring. New species arise because of this genetic adjustment that is stronger and able to thrive. English philosopher and sociologist Herbert Spencer (1820–1903) brought this idea to theories about human interaction. The appeal of Spencer's version of sociology rested largely on his use of evolutionary theory to explain social change. Spencer said change occurs in societies as their members adapt to changes in their environments, whether changes in the natural environment or in the social environment. In developing his theory of social evolution, Spencer borrowed heavily from the work of Darwin, and as a result, his theory came to be known as *social Darwinism*. According to Spencer, the fact that humans, unlike other species, have remained similar even on different continents must be explained by the fact that we adapt to changes in our environment through the use of culture rather than through biological adaptation. This process, which can be termed social evolution, parallels biological evolution in that the most successful adaptations are handed down to the next generation. It is this process that Spencer had in mind when he used the phrase "survival of the fittest." He meant that the people who are most successful at adapting to the environment in which they find themselves are most likely to survive and have children who will also be successful.

Darwin's theory inspired a revolution in social thought. Sociologist and social philosopher William Graham Sumner (1840–1910) based his theory of society on humans' need to adapt to an environment of scarcity. When resources, especially land, were plentiful there would be peace and institutions based on democratic forms of government could flourish. But eventually, when population growth made it necessary to distribute the same amount of resources among more people, societies would lean toward oligarchy (rule by the most powerful) and greater use of coercion and force. Sumner introduces the terms *folkways* and *mores* to sociology. These were cultural forms of social control that provide guidelines for competition and survival. We address these cultural forms and connect them to our development of a moral code. Folkways and mores are the basis of law.

Perhaps we can end as we began, with a melding of the wisdom of the ancients with the modern day. Aristotle as well as the American founding father James Madison recognized that society is made up of differing social groups with differing interests. With institutions such as a divided government (for example: state versus central, legislative/executive/judicial branches), it would be difficult for one faction to gain control of all aspects of society. Thus it is a government based on the separation of powers. The result is a society that no one faction could take over, and any action can find allies to help defend it from alliances of factions. However, it is not so modern; it is Polybius and Cicero building on Aristotle.

Theory is structured social thought that we impose on random events in order to make sense of chaos. Regardless of the variations in how theorists define conflict, one thing to keep in mind is that conflict management is a process. It is not static; rather it must be flexible and constantly assessing whether it is productive and effective.

2.1 APPLIED EXERCISE: GROUP PROJECT BASED ON THE SEVEN CORE ELEMENTS USED TO PREPARE FOR A SUCCESSFUL NEGOTIATION

Group Project Rubrics—The SEVEN ELEMENTS
1. Students are divided into groups to analyze *a conflict of interest to the group*:
2. Students are to use the course materials to analyze a conflict of interest to them
3. Students will present their findings during the last week of the semester
4. The group will hand in an outline of the general information facts of the case that identifies:

- parties and their **relationships**
- the **communication**: people and purpose (identify different conversations)
- **interests** (needs/concerns) of each party
- **options** (brainstorming)
- **legitimacy** (laws, codes, standards relevant to options)
- elements of the **agreement**
    - Who has the authority to agree?
    - Is there a commitment—when? At what level?
    - Is it tentative, firm, signed?
- the **alternative**: what is the exit strategy or walkaway for each party?
    - (BATNA: best alternative to a negotiated agreement—for yourself and for the other[s])

2.2 APPLIED EXERCISE: ANALYSIS OF GROUP AS THEY WORKED ON THE CLASS PROJECT

GROUP PROCESS: APPLICATION OF THE FUNCTIONAL ANALYSIS OF HOW THE MEMBERS OF YOUR GROUP WORK ON THE ASSIGNED PROJECT; THAT IS, WHAT THEIR ROLES ARE.

Functionalism: Four functional problems that must be solved in order for a system to survive long term: 1) Adaptation; 2) Goal Attainment; 3) Integration; and 4) Pattern Maintenance.

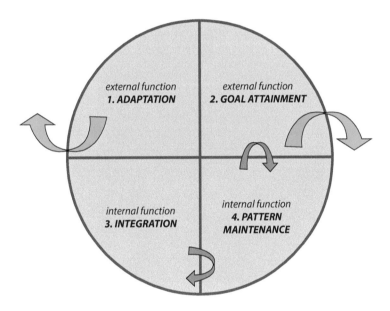

Fig. 2.1 Functionalism: Four Functional Problems

Process Paper: participant observation of your term-project group

- Who is the adapter?
- Who is responsible for attaining the group's goals?
- Who is the integrator?
- Who is responsible for maintaining the group's patterns?
- Describe how your group has functioned.
- What do you think about the outcome of the group's effort?

NOTES

1. Coser, L.A. *The Functions of Social Conflict.* New York: The Free Press. 1956, 8.
2. "Discourse on the Arts and Sciences" and "Discourse in Inequality." Following this Rousseau praised what he called the "noble savage": primitive man unspoiled by terrible things like education and society.
3. See James A. Schellenberg's text, *Conflict Resolution: Theory, Research, and Practice,* 1996.
4. Weber, Max (1947). *The Theory of Social and Economic Organization* (A. M. Henderson and T. Parsons, Trans.). New York: Free Press, 152.
5. Note: See Diagram 2.2 in this text—we will outline an activity that illustrates the functional paradigm. Students in our classes are required to complete a team project to be presented at the end of the term. They are required to analyze their group by assessing how each member functioned on the team. Using the four functional problems adaptation, integration, pattern maintenance, and goal attainment, they all write a process paper.
6. W. I. Thomas and his colleague, Polish sociologist Florian Znaniecki, conducted the first major comparative study of American sociology, *The Polish Peasant in Poland and America* (1927). New York: Knopf.
7. Blumer first used the term in his article for Schmitt (1937). See also Blumer, Herbert. 1969. *Symbolic Interactionism: Perspective and Method.* New York: Prentice Hall. A good survey of symbolic interactionism is Stryker, Sheldon. 1980. *Symbolic Interactionism: A Structural Version.* Menlo Park, CA: Benjamin/ Cummings.

CHAPTER 3

PRESENTATION OF RELATED SOCIAL THEORIES, SOCIAL THOUGHTS, CORE CONCEPTS, AND FUNDAMENTAL PARADIGMS USED TO FRAME OUR UNDERSTANDING OF CONFLICT

HOW DO WE MAKE JUDGMENTS ABOUT THE BEHAVIOR OF THOSE WHO ARE PART OF OUR SOCIAL NETWORK?
WHAT ARE OUR RULES FOR RELATIONSHIPS AND WHAT ARE OUR FRIENDSHIP CONTRACTS BASED ON?

Let us continue our introspective journey. Like communication, culture is ubiquitous and has a profound effect on humans. Culture is simultaneously invisible and pervasive. As we go about our daily lives, we are not overly conscious of our culture's influence. Yet most of our feelings and behaviors are connected to culture.

Culture can be seen as a system of norms, a system of rules. Every culture includes a wide array of norms that constitute a system of social control. Norms are never absolute. There are always conditions under which they may be violated. How we feel about the violation of some rules is important to consider. Our feelings prioritize norms for us so we can internalize certain rules while ignoring others.

Societies are the people and culture is the way people of a society behave. Societies are populations organized to carry out major functions of life. A society's culture consists of all the ways in which its members think about their society and communicate about it among themselves. We can also define *culture* as all the modes of thought, behavior, and production that are handed down from one generation to the next by speech, gestures, writing, buildings, and all other communication among humans. Culture is learned behaviors that are integrated by a group, shared among group members, and passed along. These behaviors become a way of life, which are the customs and beliefs that distinguish one group from another. Therefore, human performance is dependent upon culture that provides a framework for analyzing interactions. A useful framework for thinking about culture is in viewing it as ideas (ways of thinking that organize consciousness) and norms (accepted ways of doing or carrying out ideas). Keep in mind that the wide array of norms (rules) constitutes a system of social control and is connected to your moral code.

Each of us tends to view others' behavior in terms of our own background, so that actions that may appear to us as strange, bizarre, or deviant may be acceptable and normal by those outside our cultural group. Also, remember that norms (rules) are never absolute. The rules labeled as folkways are less sanctioned (rewarded or punished for adhering to or violating norms) and we have weak feelings about the violation of these norms. The rules that are labeled mores are considered vital for the continuation of the group and society. We have strong feelings about the violation of mores.[1] Laws are norms that have been enacted through the formal procedures of government. Laws often formalize the mores of a society by putting them in written form and interpreting them.

It is important to recognize how we feel about certain norms. This will directly relate to how we internalize them. In understanding ourselves in relationships, we need to become aware of our rules, our contracts. I like to begin each semester with an assignment to analyze two failed friendships. The failures point to the rules of your friendship contracts. Awareness of our rules for our relationships gives us insight into our moral code. When we have *strong feelings* about the violation of a norm, then we attach *right and wrong* to certain related actions. When there is right and wrong attached, we are talking about *morals*.

3.1 APPLIED EXERCISE: CULTURE—A NORMATIVE SYSTEM

This typology of norms describes graphically the components involved in the process in which individuals internalize their moral code. Think about your culture.

- Why do we feel strongly about some rules and not about others?
- When we have strong feelings about the violation of certain rules, we attach right and wrong to them. This becomes our moral code. Why did you break off from that friend?
- What relationship rule(s) was/were violated?
- Discuss your feelings about your relationship rules.

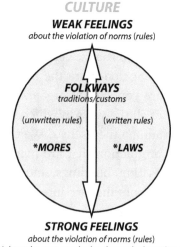

Fig. 3.1 Weak-Strong Feelings

3.2 APPLIED EXERCISE: RELATIONSHIP CONTRACTS

A history of two failed friendships with an analysis of the rules of the friendship: what was the original contract and what exactly was violated?

Consider two failed friendships you have had in your life. Focus on a same-sex relationship and an opposite-sex relationship. Outline how you met, what the foundation of your relationship was, and why you aren't friends anymore.

Essay

Briefly give the history of two failed friendships:

- First, a same-sex friend
- Second, an opposite-sex friend

Be sure to include:

- a *beginning*: what drew you together/what were the elements that attracted you to that person?
- a *middle*: what were the things that bound the friendship/what kept you together?
- an *end*: what split you up/what ended the relationship?

Debrief

- What are the rules of your friendship contracts?
- What got violated?
- Did you have different rules for your male friends and female friends?
- Do you have different relational rules for older/younger, educated, professional, handsome/beautiful, etc.?

NOTES

1. The terms *mores* and *folkways* were used by William Graham Sumner in his study *Folkways*, 1940/1907, Boston: Ginn.

2. This is to examine the rules or contract we have with others.

CHAPTER 4

UNDERSTANDING CULTURE AS A SYSTEM OF NORMS OR RULES

HOW DO VALUE PRIORITIES AND GOALS FRAME THE RULES WE INTERNALIZE?
HOW DO OUR STRONG FEELINGS ABOUT THE VIOLATIONS OF CULTURAL
NORMS CONNECT TO DEVELOPING OUR MORAL CODE?

Culture for our purposes is defined as a system of norms or rules in a feedback relationship with the individual preference system (our values and our goals).

From a helpless, entirely self-centered being, the human infant develops into a person capable of performing roles in a wide variety of groups. Those groups evolve and change. This part of the book covers the individual's preference system, the system that selects, prioritizes, and internalizes our cultural norms (rules). This process of socialization enables individuals to become participating members of groups and of society. Keep in mind that groups are as small as dyads (two-member groups) or triads (three-member groups). Our values, goals, and attitudes are critical in the internalization of norms. These values, goals, and attitudes make up what can be called your individual preference system.

In studying conflict management, our main interest is in the self and society. To examine this perspective, we will turn to theories proposed by Sigmund Freud, George Herbert Mead, and Charles Horton Cooley. Additionally, cognitive psychologist Lawrence Kohlberg's work on the levels of moral judgment has become a basis of our comprehending or deepening our understanding of what is happening to the other. Kohlberg describes individuals who are passive receivers of their moral code or active producers of their moral code.

For Freud, the creator of modern psychoanalysis, the personality or self develops out of the processes of socialization, primarily in the family. Freud divides the personality into three interrelated parts that permit the self to function well in society. These elements of the self are the id, the ego, and the superego.

The first element, everyone is born with an id. This is the part that contains the infant's unsocialized drives. The id represents self-centeredness in its purest form.

The second element, the moral codes of adults, especially parents, become part of the personality Freud calls the superego. Freud thought this part of the personality contained all the norms, values, and feelings that are taught in the socialization process.

The third vital element of the personality is what Freud describes as the ego, our conception of ourselves in relation to others; that is, our social selves. To have a strong ego is to be self-confident in dealing with others and to be able to handle criticism. According to Freud's description, those with a weak ego need continual approval from others. In the growth of the personality, according to Freud, the ego, or social part of the self, is critical and occurs only with a great deal of conflict. The conflict is between the id, basic urges, and the superego, society's need for a socialized adult. Freud describes stages that represent the development of ego functions that control the desires of the id. The conflict between the demands of the superego and the desires of the id is always threatening to disrupt the functioning of the ego. Conflict is intrapersonal, between parts of the self. It is found inside the individual. For Freud, conflict is internal.

Symbolic interactionist theories examine how the self emerges in the context of social interaction. George Herbert Mead[1] developed many of the ideas that are central to symbolic interactionism and believed strongly that the self was a social product. We are *not* born with selves that are brought out by socialization. Instead, we acquire a self by observing and assimilating the identities of others. Language is the way we identify and assimilate the identities of others. Influenced by educational philosopher John Dewey and psychologist William James, Mead believed that the stimulus-response model of learning proposed by behaviorists like Watson was an incomplete explanation of how socialization takes place. It could not account for the ways in which humans manipulate symbols, or for the different levels of meaning that can be communicated through language and gesture. Mead argues that the emergence of self could arise only through the use of language. As Mead

Self = center of the flower
("*I*" and "**ME**")

Petals = our **group memberships**

Fig. 4.1 Sunflower

Adapted from Copyright © Jeffrey Rea (CC by 3.0) at https://commons.wikimedia.org/wiki/File:VallejoSunflower.jpg.

wrote, "There neither can be nor could have been any mind or thought without language; and the early stages of development of language must have been prior to the development of mind or thought."[2] Mead's view of the emergence of the self identifies culture as the center of the formation of the self. The kind of person we become is a cultural construct. Conflict is outside the self; it is in society (the groups that we belong to). For Mead and the symbolic interactionists, conflict is external.

A way to visualize the self: imagine a sunflower. The self is the center of the flower and each petal is a different group we belong to. Each individual learns the norms of his or her group, which is their family, friends, neighbors, work associates, school pals, religious groups, the community, state, country, etc. Each individual is the intersection point of every group he or she is a member of. Keep in mind that some groups are as small as a dyad, a two-member group, and some as large as the Western world.

PETALS: OUR GROUP MEMBERSHIPS

According to Mead, in all of our activities, we judge ourselves according to a generalized other that represents in our minds a composite of all the others in our lives. In its broadest sense, the idea of the generalized other refers to the way in which we internalize our society's norms. The generalized other is the individual's conception of the expectations and demands of society. This deals with the development of consciousness. Later we will discuss American Lawrence Kohlberg's theory of moral development, which emphasizes the cognitive aspects of moral behavior. I will outline a frame based on his theory.

4.1 APPLIED EXERCISE: GOALS, LIFELINE (GOALS ARE DREAMS WITH A DEADLINE AND A TIMETABLE)

Goals are defined as those specific things we define as desirable, good, and important in life. Values are those general things defined by our culture as desirable, good, and important. These things are important in our lives because they direct and influence our relationships. It is essential to focus on your goals and to write them down. Keep in mind that goals are dreams with a deadline and a timetable.

ASSIGNMENT: TEN-YEAR VISION[3]

Also, there is an added dimension to this assignment; a genie (a magical spirit) appears and says that for the next ten years you cannot fail. Everything you plan will succeed. In the vision you are going to write the script for your future life. Note that is not so far-fetched because we cannot truly fail unless we choose to give up!

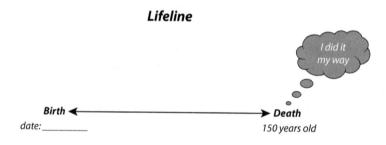

Fig. 4.2 Goals: Lifeline

1. Put your birthday under the word *Birth*
2. Place an X to mark today's date
3. Project 10 years from today
4. Describe one week (remember the rule of this vision—you cannot fail)

Describe your vision in an essay. Be as detailed as you can (describe images, smells, locations, etc.). Be sure to age everyone (family, friends, pets) in your life by ten years and put them in your vision; include:

- a description of one week 10 years from now (Monday morning through Sunday night)
- where you live (describe the environment, neighborhood, etc.)

- your marital status (if married, describe spouse)
- whether you have children (ages, sexes, etc.)
- whether or not you work (describe your job and the hours you work)
- what you do on weekends
- what you drive (describe make, model, features, etc.)

Have fun with this!

Food for thought: when considering your goals and how they affect your relationships, imagine you are planning a trip across the United States (How will you travel—by plane, RV, car, motorcycle, bicycle, or foot? Who will accompany you on this trip? How long will you take?). If you plan to go to California and your partner wants to go to Florida or Maine, then every time you move closer to your destination, you are frustrating your partner because you are moving away from their destination. You cannot genuinely celebrate their progress and they cannot honestly take pleasure in your progress. Goals can be a cause of difficult conflicts. Conflicts based on goals and values are the most difficult to resolve.

Another: use Noah's Ark as an image to explain the relevance of your goals and values. It is the time of Noah and you realize the floods are coming. You want to be with people who are heading in the same general direction. Your and their core goals and values of life must be collaborative. It is not necessary to be identical. You would want people who are ark builders, navigators, those who could take care of the animals, those who could cook, etc. Being different is good, but not on the values and goals that are important to you.

Debrief

- Look at your written list of goals and relate them to your value priority list.
- Compare and contrast your goals and values with those of the significant others in your life.

Keep in mind that they do not need to be identical, just compatible. (For example, if my intention is to travel west and my good friend wants to travel north, then I frustrate him or her when I drag us closer to my goals, and he or she frustrates me when he or she moves us closer to his or her goals.)

4.2 APPLIED EXERCISE: RANKING OUR VALUES

It is essential to know the values and priorities in your life. Also, it is important to know the value priorities of those who are an important part of your life. Keep in mind that we are a sum total of those we choose to love (love is voluntary—no one can force you to love them). So, knowing your value priorities and those of the significant people in your life is central for harmony in your primary relationships.

Value Priority: Our culture defines certain things as desirable, good, or important.

These things are important in life—we find some of them more important in our lives—they influence and direct our lives and our relationships.

We present you with a list of values considered to be motivators—all of them may be important to you, but some are more important than others. Remember, our values change as we move through our life course. Our value priorities may have been different last month, and may be different two months from now.

Read through the list thoroughly. Number these values from 1 to 15 in order of importance to you at this point in time, with 1 being most important and 15 least important:

_____ INDEPENDENCE: the opportunity to do things on your own; have freedom to do as you believe best

_____ POWER: controlling the situation around you

_____ LEADERSHIP: being able to influence others

_____ EXPERTISE: being the best in some area

_____ SELF-FULFILLMENT: having the opportunity to develop your capacities; realize your potential

_____ DUTY: doing what is expected of you

_____ NURTURING: contributing to the welfare of others

_____ FRIENDSHIP: being liked by others; having companionship

_____ FAMILY: meeting the needs of family members (security, financial, emotional)

_____ HEALTH: taking care of yourself

_____ SECURITY: not having to worry about present or future income or welfare

_____ PLEASURE: being happy and having fun

_____ WEALTH: earning a great deal of money

_____ JUSTICE: dealing with somebody or something fairly

_____ SPIRITUALITY: engaging in meaningful activity, personal growth, or blissful experience

Note: Copy this list and give it to the significant others in your life—that is, give it to the people whom you respect and seek advice from. Do not let them see your ranking until they have completed their list. Then, discuss your priorities with them and give us a summary of your analysis.

4.3 APPLIED EXERCISE: NEGOTIATING YOUR VALUES[4]

You are a member of a search-and-rescue committee appointed by the governor of New York to rescue inhabitants of the Island of Selena and take them to a specific location where they would they would begin a new life. A terrible flood has destroyed the entire village and you have received word from Command Central that there are twelve people trapped on the roof. There is room for only six individuals on your rescue vessel, and there is no telling whether or not the others can be rescued before the flood covers the roof. You have received some information on those trapped on the roof and you are required to use this information as a means for selecting your choices. Your values are your frame of reference for the exercise. After you have made your individual selection, check with the members of your group. Negotiate with the members of your group. Everyone must agree so that the six individuals chosen can be saved.

Individuals on the roof	Individual Selection	Group Consensus
1. A 36-year-old physician, known to be a racist.	✓	✓
2. A female army drill instructor; an alcoholic.		
3. A black male militant; biological researcher.	✓	
4. A male biochemist; recent immigrant.		✓
5. A female Olympic athlete; urban planner.	✓	✓
6. A film starlet; prolific writer.		
7. A third-year medical student; homosexual.	✓	✓
8. A 16-year-old girl of questionable IQ; pregnant.		
9. A 30-year-old Catholic priest; community leader.	✓	✓
10. A 22-year-old army nurse and midwife; addict.		
11. A 15-year-old boy, first-year apprentice carpenter.		
12. A 38-year-old male carpenter; served seven years for drug offenses; released three months ago.	✓	✓

Note: The population of Selena was 1,200. They are Americans who have chosen to live in their own unique world, away from the problems of "civilized" society. ⌗

NOTES

1. 1931. Mead, G.H. (1971). "Mind, Self, and Society." In M. Truzzi (ed.), *Sociology: The Classic Statements*. New York: Random House.
2. Mead, G.H. (1971). "Mind, Self, and Society." In M. Truzzi (ed.), *Sociology: The Classic Statements*. New York: Random House, 2720.
3. The best time to think about this vision is when you are in that twilight sleep, not awake and not fully asleep.
4. Source: IMCR Director Stephen Slate, Ph.D. Mediation-training exercise.

UNIT TWO

SELF-AWARENESS, APPRECIATION OF OTHERS, SELF-MOTIVATION, AND SELF-REGULATION

UNDERSTANDING CULTURE AND THE RELATIONSHIP WITH THE INDIVIDUAL PREFERENCE SYSTEM

WHY DOES GROUP MEMBERSHIP MATTER WHEN ANALYZING CONFLICT IN LIFE?
WHY IS IT IMPORTANT TO BE AWARE OF DYADIC RELATIONSHIPS, AS WELL AS GENDER, RACE, AND ETHNIC GROUP MEMBERSHIPS?

In order to understand the individual and society, we must consider roles (behavior) and status (position) in modern societies. Our identity is attached to the groups and communities to which we belong. Therefore, when focusing on roles in conflict, it is necessary to examine our group memberships because they matter.

Unlike all other animal species, humans have the capacity to live in different kinds of societies. People adapt to the world around them. Much research has been done on the subject of individual and group adaptations to new social structures of society. We will examine the relationship between you (the individual self) and society. The study of the processes whereby these adaptations occur has become an important area in the field of sociology. We use the term "society" as shorthand for many social institutions (including family, school, economic institutions, political institutions, social organizations, the courts) and our social group memberships (such as race, gender, ethnicity, class). There are two key questions: how are individuals shaped by society and how do we, in turn, shape society? ("Shape" can mean "reproduce" or "change.")

Imagine that you grew up in an agrarian or slowly industrializing society and then came to the United States, as millions of people did. A significant and probably difficult part of that experience would be getting used to the impersonality of modern American society compared to the close relationships you had with people in your native society. American society might seem to be composed of masses of strangers organized into highly impersonal categories. You would have to get used to being a shopper, a commuter, a tenant, a sports fan, a neighbor, etc. It would be necessary to shift from one to another of these roles several times a day or even several times an hour. Sociologists describe this experience as a transition from close personal relationships of our small groups and communities to impersonal relationships of a larger society. Also, a frequently used version of this distinction is derived from the American sociologist Charles H. Cooley's discussion of primary versus secondary groups. Cooley wrote about the primary group:

> I mean those characterized by intimate face-to-face association and cooperation. They are primary in several senses, but chiefly in that they are fundamental in forming the social nature and ideals of the individual. The result of intimate associations … is a certain fusion of individualities in a common whole, so that one's very self, for many purposes at least, is the common life and purpose of the group. Perhaps the simplest way of describing the wholeness is by saying "we"; it involves the sort of sympathy and mutual identification for which "we" is the natural expression.[1]

Secondary groups are groups in which we participate for a particular reason; that is, in order to accomplish a task or set of tasks. These groups are a large, usually formal, impersonal collection of people who pursue a specific goal or activity. Examples of secondary groups are college classes, political parties, professional associations, religious organizations, sports teams, labor unions, and a company's employees. It is normal not to be socially involved with members of your secondary groups. Conflict can arise from these basic perspectives.

Sociologist C. Wright Mills introduced insights that directly relate to our discussion. What we have been talking about is the idea that the individual "… can understand his own experience and guide his own fate only by locating himself within his period, that he can know his own chances in life by becoming aware of those of all individuals in his circumstances. In many ways it is a terrible lesson; in many ways it is a magnificent one."[2] Mills also said, "Neither the life of an

| **Our Social Ideas** | **Concrete** | **Filter** |
| (our social images about the world) | Observable World | (Cultural Apparatus) |

Fig. 5.1 Woman

Copyright © Depositphotos/andresr.

individual nor the history of a society can be understood without understanding both." He used the term "cultural apparatus," which can be simply described as the filter through which we view the world around us. If our lenses are tinted blue, we see the world blue. If our experiences have tinted our lenses green, then the world is seen as green.

Additionally, when considering our perceptions and conflict, there are certain social cognitive points to consider for any given communication: each party views the situation from his or her own perspective; each party has an impression of the other; each party has a view of the relationship (for example, intimate friends or casual acquaintances); each party has his or her explanation to account for their own and the other's behavior. This is using a social cognition as it relates to perception and communication. As you read this section, think about how you process and communicate your view of the world. Now think about how you develop your moral code, which include the rules that you feel strongly about. When there is a strong feeling about the violation of particular rules, we attach senses of right and wrong to them (see Chapter 3 of this text). The following figure gives the definition of culture as a normative system as it relates to our individual preference system.

CULTURE AS A NORMATIVE SYSTEM

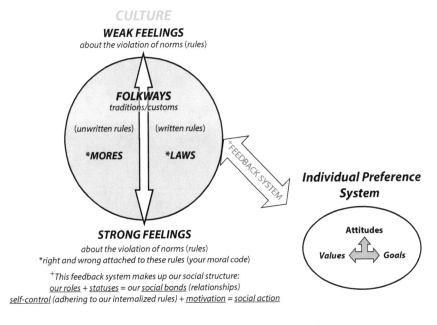

Fig. 5.2 Weak-Strong Feelings + Individual Preference System

Note: See APPLIED EXERCISES 4.1 Goals and 4.2 Values of this text.

Our individual preference system (attitudes, values, and goals) enables us to internalize the important norms of our cultural system. In our interactions we reflect our personal backgrounds (family, heritage, gender) as well as a relational history, unique life experiences, and our perceptions of each other. Each relationship (group we belong to) creates its own identity, which differentiates it from similar relationships (groups). A relationship that works for one group may not succeed with others. Interpersonal relationships shift as people change circumstances over time. Relationships have various stages as they deepen or weaken and become less powerful and end. They develop a life of their own. Also, individuals' goals and value priorities change. We are the intersection point of all the groups we belong to. Our memberships in these groups are conscious and give us our social identity. We need to understand our lenses, priorities, and preferences.

5.1 APPLIED EXERCISE: PREFERENCES (UNDERSTANDING THE RANGE OF PREFERENCE TYPES)

Are you a plunger, a wader, or a tester?
If you came up to a pool or lake,

- Would you jump right in? You are a plunger.
- Would you slowly wet one toe at a time? You will get in the water eventually, but it will take time. You are a wader.
- Would you investigate the water (Are there fish? Is it cold? Is the chemical balance normal?) You may or may not go into the water. You are a tester.

Have the group break up into plungers, waders, and testers. Then, give them 15 minutes to discuss:

1. How it feels to be in that group
2. The advantages and disadvantages of being in their particular group
3. How they see the other two groups

Debrief

- Have each group describe how it feels to be in that group.
- Have each group give the advantages and disadvantages of being in their group.
- Have each group describe the other two groups.
- What did they learn from your group discussion?
- What surprised you when listening to the other groups' report?

NOTES

1. Cooley, Charles H. (1909). *Social Organizations: Study of the Larger Mind*. New York: Scribner's, 23.
2. Mills, C. Wright. 1959. *The Sociological Imagination*. New York: Oxford University Press.

CHAPTER 6

UNDERSTANDING A MODEL DESCRIBING STAGES NEEDED TO MOVE FROM COMMUNICATING TO A CONNECTED TRUSTING RELATIONSHIP

HOW CAN THE SIX C'S (A POWERFUL, STRAIGHTFORWARD GUIDE) HELP IN DEALING WITH TOUGH NEGOTIATIONS, ESPECIALLY WITH DIFFICULT SIGNIFICANT OTHERS, ANGRY FRIENDS, AND MEAN CO-WORKERS? HOW CAN FORGIVENESS AND REAL TRUST BE ACHIEVED BY APPLYING THESE SIX CORE STEPS THAT LIE AT THE HEART OF MOST EMOTIONALLY CHALLENGED CONFLICTS?

Understand that the stages necessary to move from communicating to a connected trusting relationship are important in the building of the relationship itself. This chapter provides a guide to analyze the important stages of a relationship: the six C's—the stages to move from simple communication (sharing of information) to a connected trusting relationship—communicating, comprehending, contracting, controlling, caring, and connecting in a trusting relationship.

A feedback system is a process in which the system regulates itself by monitoring its own output. It feeds back part of its output to itself. In sociological terms, this refers to the social structure, the recurring patterns of behavior that create relationships among individuals and groups. Your values and goals support or justify how you feel about certain norms. Our roles are the way an individual behaves in a particular status (a socially defined position in a group). Thus, our social bonds (relationships) are a result of the roles we play in life. Self-control means adhering to internal rules that enable one to manage his or her own internal state (keeping disruptive emotions and impulses in check). Self-regulation includes trustworthiness. Individuals must maintain standards of honesty and integrity. Therefore, it is critical to understand trust; that is, trust of self and trust of others. Additionally, motivation and self-control result in our social action. Motivation includes the emotional tendencies that facilitate reaching one's goals.

In the next chapter we will illustrate steps and stages that enable students to understand themselves in their social relationships. Over the years, these frames helped to articulate a real-world approach to understanding what leads to a connected trusting relationship. We will broadly discuss individuals in their relationships (social bonds) and communication.

Trust plays a vital role in every human interaction. When people are trustworthy, according to Daniel Goleman, they "act ethically and are above reproach; build trust through their reliability and authenticity; admit their own mistakes and confront unethical actions in others; and take tough, principled stands...."[1] Some additional definitions of trust are to rely upon, place confidence in, depend upon, to believe, and to charge with responsibility. When we trust, we rely on the integrity, strength, ability, surety, and ethics of a person or thing.

The emphasized opening part of community mediation training is that "Building trust is the first thing a mediator must do. When disputants arrive at a session, more often than not, they are angry with each other and distrustful."[2] In his book *Recapturing the Trust*, 2000, Bob Schachat, a colleague from the School of Business, writes: "Trust is like a butterfly, capricious and delicate. To capture a butterfly one has to use a soft net and a gentle touch."

I believe there are two considerations before I would/could/should trust someone:

- First, am I willing to open myself up and let this person in? If I am unwilling to let my guard down, then I am unwilling to trust.
- Second, am I sure about my judgment that this person will keep me safe?

Answer the two questions now. (This is the way I encourage students to think about trust in their relationships.)

My students' most common responses that arose during discussions about lost trust:

- "I was mad/angry at the person."
- "I was in disbelief and sad that the person let me down."
- "I felt stupid that I trusted them."
- "I felt sad, depressed."
- "I was angry at myself for trusting them."

What were your feelings? My point is that we open up to people we trust and we feel confident that they will keep us safe.

When the trust was violated, how did you feel about others in your network? Did you begin looking closely at others because you may not have judged them correctly, either?

An episode of broken trust affects the self-worth of an individual. People build walls around themselves to prevent being hurt again.

6.1 APPLIED EXERCISE: TRUST AND LISTENING

Activity: Trust Walk

Variations of this activity are used in management training, academic workshops, mediation programs, and counseling sessions. Students find it an important experience because it not only illustrates trusting another with your safety, but also demonstrates that we do not listen to our partner if we do not trust.

- Everyone is instructed to think of a story (something that was emotional and happened within the past year) to tell his or her partner. The story should take five minutes.
- The class is divided into dyads.
- Each pair receives a blindfold.
- Each pair should have a way to keep track of time.
- One member of the dyad is blindfolded; that person is blind and mute until the blindfold comes off.
- The blind person cannot talk or gesture.
- The sighted person is the speaker and tells their five-minute story first.
- The sighted person must keep their blind partner safe.
- The sighted person must try to give the blind partner as wide an experience as possible (there is no sitting down; they must keep moving).
- The sighted person must keep walking around, leaving the classroom.
- In five minutes the partners switch roles.
- Now the roles are reversed—the original blind person must keep his or her partner safe, tell the five-minute story, and get them back to the classroom.

Debrief

- What did it feel like to be blind?
- Did you feel safe?
- Could you concentrate on the story being told by your partner?
- Can you see a relationship between listening and trust?
- What was it like telling a story to someone mute and unable to gesture?
- How was it trying to tell your story while concerned about the safety of your partner?

Most of my students reported that they did not listen to the story when they felt unsafe. Some, who developed trust with their partners, reported they were able to listen.

How can I analyze a relationship in order to know where there are problems that are preventing a connected trusting relationship from developing?

The steps necessary to focus on in order to move from communicating to a connected trusting relationship are the six C's. These are steps one should understand in order to move parties from simply sharing information (communicating) to a connected trusting relationship. There is a steady progression in this process and no step should be skipped. The best way to understand this model is by imagining an injuring party and an injured party in conflict.

First, *communicating* with both parties. In this step there is an open communication so perceived views of each are shared. Both parties express their own view and listen to views of the other.

Second, *comprehending*, deepening understanding so both parties comprehend what is happening to the other. In this step both seek understanding by exploring backgrounds to understand how conclusions were reached. Then both revise thinking to accurately fit the new revealed reality. (This is trying to get into the other's head and trying to walk in his or her shoes.)

Third, *contracting*, understanding the rules of the relationship contract. This results in a restored sense of justice so mutually agreed-on rules can be followed. In this step, parties agree on what the relationship rules should be in light of their new understanding.

If there is convicting past behavior in terms of rules and the absence of admitting responsibility and wrong/right, then forgiveness is impossible. However, if there is an admission of responsibility and wrong/right, then forgiveness is possible. In this step, there is a commitment to make changes in relationships.

Fourth, *controlling*, restoring a sense of control so both parties can count on the other's response. In this step there is an ending of old destructive cycles and making restitution to the injured party. There is an extinguishing of old behavior and learning new.

Fifth, *caring*, restoring a sense of caring (feelings/emotions) so both parties feel the other cares about the outcome. In this step, a new constructive cycle begins because there is a release of resentments from the past. There is a restoration of good feelings for the future and a letting go of anger in order to restore the connection.

Sixth, *connecting* in a trusting relationship. In this step parties connect in order to have a relationship that they could build on where they guard against taking excessive risks that will reactivate old patterns. It is important to avoid "no trust" and "blind trust." At this point, there is a consideration of both individual perspectives from a relationship perspective. This is a strong relationship.

When there is a conflict, it helps to assess the situation by methodically analyzing the relationship step by step. Remember you should not skip a step. These stages build on one another. It is important to note that the fifth step, caring, is very critical in this process. If either party does not care about the issue or the outcome, then the relationship is doomed. There is no way of fixing this. Reaching a connected trusting relationship is *not* possible. The parties need to realize that there needs to be an entire redefinition of the relationship. Forcing things would result in a no-trust or false-trust (failed) relationship.

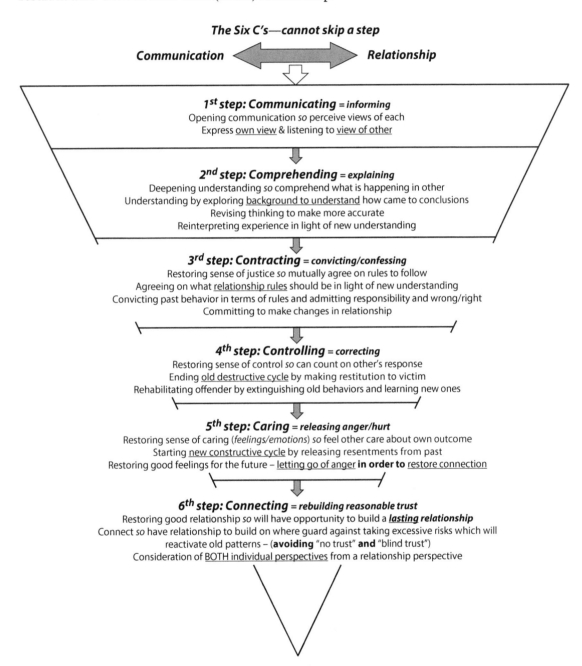

Fig. 6.1 The Six C's

6.2A APPLIED MODEL: BASED ON THE SIX C'S MODEL, ARE FORGIVENESS AND JUSTICE POSSIBLE?

Forgiveness is difficult to deal with because of the value questions that are raised. Yet they are central issues in relationships where there has been pain. The aim is to outline a model based on the six C's that explains ways to resolve these issues by integrating an understanding of moral development.

The model describes useful ways to manage this process. See figure 6.2 below:

Forgiveness and Justice

INJURING PERSON   INJURIOUS BEHAVIOR   INJURED PERSON

There must first be an understanding of
"the problem" that inclined the person to behave in this way.
What is the nature of "the problem"?

Problems NOT requiring forgiveness		*Problems requiring forgiveness*
if injuring person is not aware of the impact of their behavior, then it can be resolved by communication…	**COMMUNICATING**	*if injuring person is aware impact of their behavior…*
if the injuring person heard the other's message but did not understand it…	**COMPREHENDING**	*if the injuring person heard and understands the other's message…*
if the injuring person understands but disagrees about whether the behavior is appropriate, that is, what are the acceptable expectations for the relationship…	**CONTRACTING**	*if the injuring person knows the expectation or agreement for the relationship…*
if the injuring person knows what the right behavior is but finds it difficult to act accordingly…	**CONTROLLING**	*if the injuring person chooses to willfully violate the relationship expectations…*

If the injuring person does not care about injuring the other, then it is not possible to skip to a connected trusting relationship. Without caring for the damage this violation will/has caused to the other, then the other person is likely to feel deeply angry and hurt.

CARING

In this case there need to be a "healing of feelings" of injustice, exploitation and uncaring. A positive, trusting relation cannot be restored unless the parties are willing to begin communicating with the NEW awareness of feelings and emotions.

CONNECTING in a trusting relationship

Fig. 6.2 Are Forgiveness and Justice Possible?

Communicating (informing) to present the wrong (the feelings wheel, how to raise an issue, outlined in the next chapter). This step is aimed at opening communication, expressing your view, and listening to the view of the other. Your paraphrasing and reframing skills are important.

> *Problem*: the angry, attacking, avenging person could only indict.
> *Problem*: the anxious, avoiding, appeasing person could only ignore or overlook.

Comprehending (explaining) to determine the wrong. This step is aimed at deepening understanding so both parties can comprehend what happened to the other. It is important to explore backgrounds to understand conclusions; revise thinking to make it more accurate; and reinterpret experiences, responsibilities, and outcomes in light of new understanding.

> *Problem*: the angry, attacking, avenging person could only blame.
> *Problem*: the anxious, avoiding, appeasing person could only give excuses.

Contracting (convicting/confessing) to admit the wrong. This step is aimed at restoring a sense of justice. Both parties agree on the rules to follow. It is at this point that both agree what the rules of the relationship will be in light of the new understanding. Also, there is a convicting of past behavior in terms of the rules and admitting wrong and responsibility, with a commitment to make changes in the relationship.

> *Problem*: the angry, attacking, avenging person could only indict.
> *Problem*: the anxious, avoiding, appeasing person could only condone and/or justify.

Controlling (correcting) to correct the wrong. This step is aimed at restoring a sense of control so both parties can count on each other's response. At this point, there is a genuine effort to end the old destructive cycle by making restitution to the injured party through repairing, repaying, or retribution. The goal is to rehabilitate the offender by extinguishing old behaviors and learning new ones.

> *Problem*: the angry, attacking, avenging person could only punish.
> *Problem*: only the anxious, avoiding, appeasing person could pardon.

Caring (discovering love and trust) to release the wrong. This step is aimed at restoring a sense of caring so both parties feel the other cares about outcomes. At this point, there is a starting of a constructive cycle by releasing resentments from the past through forgiveness. This is the restoring of love for the future … this is the celebrating of reborn love and trust.

Problem: the angry, attacking, avenging person could only retain old anger.
Problem: the anxious, avoiding appeasing person could only recover the fantasy of old love.

Connecting (rebuilding) to rebuild a trusting relationship. This step is aimed at restoring trust in the relationship where both parties guard against taking excessive risks that will reactivate old destructive patterns. However, this includes realistic trust and enables risk-taking opportunities to try new patterns.

Problem: the angry, attacking, avenging person has no trust.
Problem: the anxious, avoiding, appeasing person has blind trust.

The definitions of forgiveness vary. My definition of forgiveness is to cease to feel debilitating anger, resentment, and hatred against the offender. Forgiveness is not an easy thing—whether you are the person who needs to offer forgiveness or the person who needs to be forgiven. Remember that to forgive does not mean to forget.

Often the first step toward forgiveness is an apology. Apologies may be necessary to resolve conflicts when the rights of others have been violated. Apologies can repair relationships if the steps of the six C's are dissected. Research has suggested that an apology is needed before the relationship can be renegotiated. There have been studies that suggest apologies help reduce both the punishment the perpetrator receives and the anger the victim experiences. Even after the words are spoken and accepted, and time has passed, true forgiveness is difficult. Keep in mind that there are some hurts that we can let go of, which fly away like dust in the wind. There are others that are carved in stone in our memories. These are the deep hurts that are not merely mile markers in our life's journey, but are major shifts in our life's direction. These deep hurts impact the living present from a dead past. A loved one's murder, a close friend's betrayal, an abusive parent, or a spouse's infidelities are hurts that do not heal with the passage of time. Anger, resentment, revenge, and chronic stress can destroy us physically, psychologically, and spiritually. The six C's offer a structured process possibly to help us reframe the experience and rewrite the contract with the offending person in order to connect with a realistic sense of trust and be able to get on with life. There is a complex nature of the offender/offended relationship. It is important to consider the role of both the offender and the forgiver. When we have been hurt, we can be destroyed by our resentment or we can consider forgiving. Resentment will destroy personal well-being.

If this dynamic interpersonal process is followed, step by step, there is an opportunity for movement toward a trusting, functional, connected relationship. Thus, we see that the decision to forgive is based on the need to conceptualize this dynamic process. There is a need to restore reasonable trust based on reality and respect. This must include an understanding of justice and fairness.

The individual's moral code is the basis of this understanding. Lawrence Kohlberg and others have studied the understanding of moral reasoning and levels of moral judgment. There is much research on cognitive development and the complexity of these social processes. In Chapter 8 of this text, there is a model based on Kohlberg's level of moral judgment that adds an important dimension to our understanding of the elements of the six C's. However, it is important to be able to openly communicate with the other party. Therefore, the next chapter will outline steps for raising tough issues while being sensitive to others' feelings.

6.2B APPLIED EXERCISE: FORGIVENESS

- Identify an episode of forgiveness in your own life: describe *injuring person*, *injurious behavior*, and *injured person*.
- Assess the episode using 6.2A APPLIED MODEL the steps of the six C's.
- Compare and contrast different forgiveness episodes: family, friends, dating relationships.

NOTES

1. D. Goleman. (1998). *Working with Emotional Intelligence*. New York: Bantam Books, 89–90.
2. Steven Slate. *Mediation Training Manual*. (1999). IMCR Resolution Center Dispute, 16.

CHAPTER 7

FEELINGS WHEEL

How to begin to communicate:

- Understand the basic steps in raising an issue
  - focus: appreciation of self and the other, including feelings
- Understand the importance of the self-worth, self-awareness, and how we see the world in trusting connected relationships
  - focus: how to prepare to share information (open communication)

Let us consider a significant conflict we might have with someone important to us.

Think about how many confusing conversations you have experienced lately. Why did communication break down in those conversations? Effective communication involves mutual understanding and a clear definition of issues. This must begin with you and how you view the problem. You need to have a clear picture of your perception of the event in question. Perception is the process by which we filter and interpret what our senses tell us in order to create a meaningful picture of the event. Each one of us has our set of lenses or filters through which we view the world. You do not see the world exactly the same as others, nor do you see absolutely everything differently. Therefore, you need to have a well-defined, accurate, clear-cut picture in your mind in order to share it with the other.

Communication is the first step of the six C's and it is key to resolving conflict. However, communication is itself often the cause of conflict. Successful communication is the ability to verbally exchange our ideas, feelings, perceptions, and conceptions about a particular topic. In order to share information, you must first raise the issue with the other party. It is important to unambiguously frame the dispute in your own mind. This takes preparation and thought; therefore, I offer this six-point model in order to simplify a complex, often emotion-laden process. The model enables you to step back from the conflict event and appreciate yourself and your relationship with the other. This is necessary for both parties to become open in their communication, their exchange of information.

Consider the first three steps of the six Cs: Communicating, Comprehending, and Contracting. When we analyze a conflict relationship, it is important to look at *the communication* or the sharing of information before we can comprehend the different sides of the argument. It is vital to understand how to raise an issue.

To properly raise a tough/sensitive issue while being sensitive to the other's feelings, we should consider these six points:

- **SELF-AWARENESS/SELF-WORTH**: What do I appreciate about myself? What do I appreciate about the other? This is the MOST important step and the foundation that makes an open dialogue possible. (See the Self-Appreciation activity.)
- **SENSING**: What do I see? What do I hear?
- **ANALYZING**: What do I think?
- **EMOTION**: What do I feel about what I think?
- **WANTING**: What specifically do I want?
- **ACTING**: What I am going to do? At this point you are ready to begin to communicate.

Successfully raising an issue begins with self-appreciation. Unless an individual has self-worth, there is little chance that he or she will open up. It is critical that the views of both parties are openly and freely expressed. Additionally, I suggest planning carefully when you are going to raise the issue. Make sure both parties are ready to listen. Select a time and place that will not be interrupted by phone, people, radio, TV, or any other distraction.

A suggestion for staging the conversation: If it is personal and intimate, you may suggest a 45-minute break to get lunch or coffee. This way, you can raise the issue, stop and eat, and have time to be together to talk on the way home. Also, sitting in the car looking forward can make it easier to initiate the conversation.

7.1 APPLIED EXERCISE: SELF-APPRECIATION AND OTHER APPRECIATION

FIRST STEP OF THE SIX STEPS OF THE FEELINGS WHEEL

PART ONE: SELF-APPRECIATION

- Think about your best friend (could be a family member).
- Think about how you communicate with this person.
- Write down three reasons this person is lucky to have you in his or her life.

Debrief

- Recognize the character traits that you possess.
- Own those competencies.
- Appreciate your self-worth. [*A classic movie from 1946,* It's a Wonderful Life, *tells the story of a man who looks at how the world would have been if he had never been born. George Bailey learns to appreciate himself and has an improved self-worth. I highly recommend watching this film.*]

PART TWO: APPRECIATION OF THE OTHER

- Think about the other party.
- Think about how you communicate with this person (what connects you to him or her?).
- Write down three reasons you are lucky to have this person in your life.

Debrief

- Recognize the character traits he or she possesses.
- Recognize and appreciate his or her personal character traits and competencies.
- Recognize why you respect this person.
- Focus on this person and your relationship before the conflict occurred.

Now, the parties are able to express their own views and listen to the views of the other. This is particularly important in situations where there is an imbalance of status/power. Respecting yourself and respecting the other will allow open and meaningful communication between the parties.

7.2 APPLIED EXERCISE: FEELINGS WHEEL, RAISING AN ISSUE

This is a step-by-step preparation with awareness of your feelings (note: do not skip any of these critical points).

Questions: Identify and describe a difficult issue you were faced with. How would you apply the six points to raising that issue? What is your description of how you would begin to communicate?

Discussion: The next time you find yourself in a conflict, go through these six points in your mind before you approach the other person. I promise you that it really works because it enables you to think deeply about the issue while considering your feelings. Remember that your *feelings* are the specific way you translate your emotions. Feelings are very personal and tie directly into our identity. As humans, we all have emotions; however, the way we outwardly express our emotion is based on our life experience. No one can tell you how you should feel.

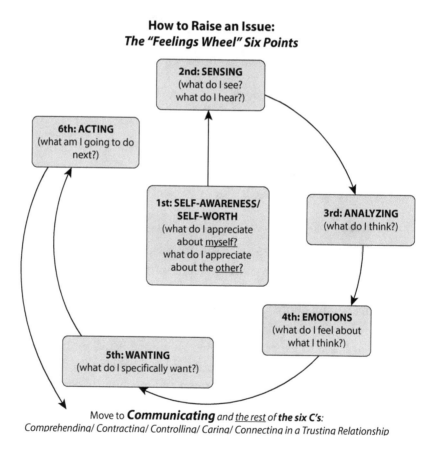

How to Raise an Issue:
The "Feelings Wheel" Six Points

2nd: SENSING (what do I see? what do I hear?)

6th: ACTING (what am I going to do next?)

1st: SELF-AWARENESS/ SELF-WORTH (what do I appreciate about <u>myself?</u> what do I appreciate about the <u>other?</u>)

3rd: ANALYZING (what do I think?)

4th: EMOTIONS (what do I feel about what I think?)

5th: WANTING (what do I specifically want?)

Move to ***Communicating*** *and <u>the rest</u> of **the six C's***: *Comprehending/ Contracting/ Controlling/ Caring/ Connecting in a Trusting Relationship*

Fig. 7.1 How to Raise an Issue: The "Feelings Wheel" Six Points

Here's a general experience, a scenario that might explain why men are stereotyped as not communicating their feelings with others. Think about how mothers raise their sons. Imagine: Your son is fighting with his younger sibling because of a broken toy (justified anger in his mind). He may yell, "I want to kill you! I hate you! I want you to die!" (or something equally vicious and mean). It is necessary for a good parent to break up the fight and tell the boy to go to his room until he can act like a good older brother. So, he retreats to his room with his anger and resentment. He knows he cannot get out of his confinement until he masks his true feelings and pretends he is polite and well behaved. When he comes out he may pretend to express the appropriate feelings toward his sibling. This boy learns to suppress his true feelings and mask them with the correct expression. When he grows into manhood and his girlfriend asks him to tell her how he is feeling, he probably has no clue what she is talking about. He was trained to suppress his true feelings and express only the politically correct responses. [A parent cannot allow the child to threaten violence, but an approach is to validate the anger (his feelings) and explain that he will come to realize the severity of his reaction is really over the top. The parent could offer some suggestions to enable him to calm down.] I believe that the hand that rocks the cradle rules the world. We, their mothers, have created the men who do not openly and freely express their true feelings because they were usually rewarded for quashing them and faking those they did express. This could be why men don't communicate their feelings in the same way many women expect.

CHAPTER 8

MORAL JUDGMENT AND THE PSYCHOLOGICAL MUSCLE THAT ENHANCES MORAL DECISION-MAKING

WHY IS IT IMPORTANT TO UNDERSTAND HOW WE MAKE OUR MORAL JUDGMENTS?
HOW IS THIS MORAL DECISION-MAKING RELATED TO MANAGING CONFLICT?
WHAT COMPETENCIES ARE NEEDED TO ENHANCE OUR MORAL DECISION-MAKING?

Moral development depends on people's concepts of justice. People's concept of justice depends on their sense of right and wrong. This can be defined as their understanding of the reason that a rule has to be followed.

Wisdom is knowing one's self. Emotional intelligence, the psychological muscle, is the capacity for recognizing our own feelings and those of others, for motivation of ourselves, and for managing emotions in ourselves and in our relationships.

MORAL JUDGMENT AND THE PSYCHOLOGICAL MUSCLE THAT ENHANCES MORAL DECISION-MAKING

Understanding our moral code and moral decision-making are the emphases of this chapter. This introspective book to managing conflict is a guided tour to discovering and verifying the self in order to successfully assess others in our relationships (using the six C's—see Chapter 6 of this text). We see others though our lenses; therefore, our values, goals, and attitudes are critical. These values, goals, and attitudes make up our individual preference system (see Chapters 3 and 4 of this text). Our preference system enables us to internalize the norms or rules that we feel strongly about. When we feel strongly about certain rules or norms, we attach senses of right and wrong to them (we feel strongly about the violation of these norms or rules). These particular norms or rules make up our moral code (see Chapter 5 of this text). We need to live in the present and deal with the realities of our life here and now. The work of personal development begins by centering yourself (self-appreciation and self-worth) in order to be able to practice self-observation. As each individual learns and internalizes the norms or rules of our culture, a unique self is formed. This is our conception of the expectations of society and its demands. (According to G.H. Mead, we judge ourselves according to a generalized other that represents in our minds a composite of all the significant others in our lives—see Chapter 2 of this text.)

Knowing your moral code and understanding how it has evolved can help you learn how to bring positive change into your life through successfully negotiating and mediating. It can help clarify the way you relate to yourself and others in relationship contracts. The moral decision-making model allows you to observe yourself in the midst of your daily life. It gives you a greater understanding of how you handle the circumstances and issues you and others face. This presents you with the challenge of courageously observing yourself as you really are. In the act of seeing yourself objectively, you will find yourself in a state of increased transparency in which to discover and assess your moral judgments. This gives you the ability to see yourself as you are and understand the tint of your lenses.

This chapter is focused on the moral decision-making. Actually, in the social world, it is that which forms the conscious of thinking people. Jean Piaget[1] was one of the original thinkers who researched and wrote about children's cognitive and moral development. He was concerned with how children understand their environment, how they view the world, and how they develop their personal philosophies. Piaget was able to generalize his findings into a set of cognitive stages that roughly describe the intellectual development of the normal child, just as Sigmund Freud and Erik Erikson's stages describe emotional development. The final phase of Piaget's work dealt with children's moral reasoning—the way children interpret the rules of games and judge the consequences of their actions. This line of investigation has been advanced by American social psychologist Lawrence Kohlberg, whose research incorporates Piaget's approach to the development of children's notions of morality.

Kohlberg's theory of moral development emphasizes the cognitive aspects of moral behavior. In a study of 57 Chicago children that began in 1957 and continued until the children were young adults, Kohlberg developed a theory of moral development consisting of three stages:

- first, the *pre-conventional*, in which the child acts out of desire for reward and punishment;
- second, *conventional*, in which the child's decisions are based on an understanding of right and wrong as embodied in social rules and laws; and
- third, *post-conventional*, in which the individual develops a sense of relativity and can distinguish between social laws and moral principles.

The pre-conventional and the conventional stages can be described as passively receiving their moral code. The post-conventional stage can be described as actively producing their moral code; being part of creating their rules for conduct.[2] Kohlberg's theory has met with criticism because it fails to account adequately for cultural difference and for differences in the moral development of males and females. Carol Gilligan addresses this point.

However, I have based (with some variations noted in the model) the following chart on Kohlberg's model of the levels of moral development. This is useful in assessing our relationships by using the six C's (see Chapter 6 of this text).

In my model, <u>Stage 1: Personal Preference</u> is the lowest level of moral judgment. Other people establish the rules. Think about a child who chooses to follow certain rules because of fear of punishment or promise of reward. Think about the myth of Santa at Christmas bringing gifts to good boys and girls, and lumps of coal to bad children.

<u>Stage 2: Personal Relationship</u> is a level higher in moral decision-making. The rules are still established by others. At this level we decide to do the right thing because we do not want to upset or displease people in our social network. We strive to maintain their good feeling and relationships. Also, we are concerned that we could be labeled by the action that violates these rules. Has your mother ever said, "Don't do that! What would the neighbors think?"

<u>Stage 3: Social Authority</u> is a higher level, but still the rules are established by others. These people are considered to be in positions of authority. Breaking the rules defies the authority structure and shows disrespect for authority structure.

These three levels are part of Kohlberg's pre-conventional and conventional stages.

<u>Stage 4: Social Consensus</u> is the level where the rules are established by agreement of people in your social group. At this level you are not merely a passive receiver of your moral code (like in stages 1, 2, and 3). Now (in stages 4, 5, and 6), there is a big leap in becoming an active producer of your moral code. At this level, violation of these rules will show disrespect for group standards.

<u>Stage 5: Reasoned Relational Principles</u> is another level of rules that are established through agreement; however, these rules are based on abstract principles reached through logical reasoning. People talk about aesthetic beauty, God, the good ....

<u>Stage 6: Natural Relational Principles</u> is the top level for the active producers of their moral code. This level considers the system's consequences of violation of rules because if you break a rule then you would be modeling a destructive pattern that will harm the system. At this stage there is concern for the entire social system. Violations could be considered as introducing a cancer into the system.

I believe that there are these six stages of development (no stage can be skipped).

At the lower levels, rules are understood from an egocentric point of view. The passive receivers of their moral code face the consequences imposed by a system that is beyond their control (similar to Kohlberg's pre-conventional and the conventional stages).

ACTIVE PRODUCER OF THE MORAL CODE

Stage 6 ⟺ ***Natural Relational Principles*** = rules are established *by* learning the <u>natural consequences</u> of interactional relationship systems. *If* you break the rule, you will be causing destructive consequences for the entire social system.
(*Kohlberg's Stage 6: Universal Ethical Principles*)

Stage 5 ⟺ ***Reasoned Relational Principles*** = rules are established *by* abstracting principles through <u>reasoning</u> which are used to guide rule making. *If* you break the rule, you will be violating these principles and will see self as an unethical person.
(*Kohlberg's Stage 6: Universal Ethical Principles*)

Stage 4 ⟺ ***Social Consensus*** = rules are established *by* <u>agreement</u> of people in a group. *If* you break the rule, you will defy what the group has established, and the group will punish you to teach you to respect group standards.
(*Kohlberg's Stage 5: Social Contract or Utility and Individual Rights*)

Stage 3 ⟺ ***Social Authority*** = rules are established *by* people given <u>rule-making authority</u>. *If* you break the rule, you will defy what authority has said, and authority will punish you to teach you to respect the authority structure.
(*Kohlberg's Stage 4: Social System and Conscience*)

Stage 2 ⟺ ***Personal Relationship*** = rules are established *by* people in order to <u>maintain their good feelings and relationship</u>. *If* you break the rule, you will displease people, and they will not like you or maintain their relationship with you.
(*Kohlberg's Stage 3: Mutual Interpersonal Relationships and Conformity*)

Stage 1 ⟺ ***Personal Preference*** = rules are established *by* people according to their <u>preferences</u>. *If* you break the rule, you will upset their preferences, and they will punish you to defend their <u>interests</u>.
(*Kohlberg's Stage 2: Individualism, Instrumental Purpose, and Exchange*)

PASSIVE RECEIVER OF THE MORAL CODE

Fig. 8.1 Six Stages of Development

At the higher levels, rules are understood from the perspective of the other person and the social system. The active producers of their moral code face consequences that influence the way the social system functions (similar to Kohlberg's post-conventional stage).

Carol Gilligan[3] argues that male development has been used as a model of normal development in the theories of Freud, Erikson, Piaget, and Kohlberg. Any variation in women tended to be viewed as a variation from the normal. Thus, Freud thought of women as having a less well-developed sense of justice and being more willing to submit to life's demands than to resist them, as men might do. Erikson believed that during adolescence, the crisis or central development problem is to create an autonomous, industrious self. But girls hold their development in check as "they prepare to attract a man by whose name they will be known" (Gilligan, 1982,

12). Piaget stated that children learn morality and respect by playing games with many rules, and that because boys play such games more often, they develop a higher moral character and become more assertive; she adds that Kohlberg believes boys learn to take roles as rule makers and disputants in competitive games. Gilligan notes that these theories are based mainly on studies of boys and men and on assumptions that masculine traits are more desirable than feminine traits. As a result, she believes the goal of the study is to explain why the socialization of women fails to make them as "good" as men.

Think about shifting the focus on the advantageous qualities of the female gender identity. Then, we would wonder why men don't possess those qualities in a greater abundance. Gilligan points to an empirical study by the sociologist Janet Lever (1976, 1978) of 181 primary school children and their school games. Keep in mind that several social scientists, including Mead and Piaget, agree that much social development occurs in the games of children as they learn to take on the roles of others and see themselves through others' eyes. Lever found gender differences in children's games and role taking. Boys play outdoors more often than girls. Boys play more competitive games that require more complex motor skills, like baseball and football. Girls tend to play more games that emphasize sharing, turn taking, and repetition, like jump rope. She found that boys often argue in the course of their games yet rarely end the game. Girls' arguments are fewer, but when they do occur, they usually end the game. In games, Gilligan argues that women learn to feel empathy for a friend and thus protect the friend's feelings by ending the game and leaving behind the taunts of others. In this way, Gilligan believes that women become adept at the skills of maintaining relationships and expressing emotions, whereas men become more skilled at remaining autonomous while advancing the needs of the group or team. Throughout their lives, as a result, women have difficulty being separate, individual, and assertive.

At a workshop, Gilligan described a caring voice and a just voice that everyone possesses. She argued that the caring voice is encouraged in girls during their development and that the just voice is rewarded in boys. As we look at contemporary society, there is more of a gender-neutral emphasis. This is an area of interest and for future study. However, now I would like to describe the competencies useful in becoming an active producer of our moral codes. In my opinion an important contribution includes the research of Daniel Goleman on emotional intelligence. I believe his work is very important and offers a model that should be followed in order to achieve ascendency toward the higher levels of moral judgment. Actually, this can serve as a blueprint for successful parenting. Goleman states that everyone is born with different levels of emotional intelligence. However, the wonderful news is that emotional intelligence can be learned, that these skills can be taught.

Daniel Goleman is the creator of the concept "emotional intelligence" (EQ).[4] His pioneering works articulate five skill categories that I believe are the psychological muscle that enables an individual to move up a level in their moral judgment. Goleman's research found that the soft skills of emotional intelligence are twice as important as cognitive intelligence (IQ) and technical skills for long-term success. At best, his research shows that IQ contributes about 20% to the factors that determine life success, which leaves the remaining 80% to forces that can be defined as EQ. IQ should not be considered destiny. Actually, our view of human intelligence is far too narrow, ignoring a critical range of abilities that matter in terms of how an individual succeeds in life. Goleman's research shows that his personal and social competencies (factors he defines as EQ skills—see chart) are at work when people of high IQ flounder and those with modest IQ do surprisingly well. I encourage you to read the groundbreaking brain and behavioral research of Daniel Goleman. Our discussions of moral decision-making and levels of moral judgment entail recognizing EQ as extremely relevant in understanding how to strengthen our moral decision-making. This can have immediate benefits to our health (stress levels), our relationships, our negotiations, and our work.

- EQ outlines the personal competencies; that is, the capabilities that determine how we manage ourselves. These *intrapersonal skills* focus on knowing one's internal states, preferences, resources, and institutions.
- EQ also outlines the social competences; that is, the capabilities that determine how we manage relationships. These *interpersonal skills* focus on emotional tendencies that guide or facilitate our successful engagement in communal life.

The wonderful thing about EQ is that it can be taught and it can be learned. EQ is the capacity for recognizing our own feelings and those of others, for motivating ourselves, and for managing emotions well in ourselves and in our relationships. Childhood is a critical time for EQ development; however, it is not fixed at birth. EQ can be nurtured and strengthened throughout the life course. Goleman's books are smart and adventurous; in fact, I feel they strike a nice balance for science and common sense. EQ gives an entirely new way of looking at the root causes of many of the ills of our families, friendships, work associations, and society. This connects with using the six C's for relationship analysis. EQ is particularly relevant in the comprehending, contracting, and controlling stages (see Chapter 6 of this text).

CHART 8.1[5]

Personal Competencies

Self-Awareness: knowing one's internal states, resources, and intuitions
emotional awareness   *self-confidence*
accurate self-assessment

Self-Motivation: managing one's internal states, impulses, and resources
self-control   *adaptability*
trustworthiness   *innovation*
conscientiousness

Self-Regulation: emotional tendencies that guide or facilitate reaching goals
achievement drive   *initiative*
commitment   *optimism*

Social Competencies

Empathy: being aware of others' feelings, needs, and concerns
understanding others   *leveraging diversity*
developing others   *political awareness*
helping others

Social Skills: being adept at inducing desirable responses in others
influence   *communication*
leadership   *building bonds*
change catalyst   *collaboration*
negotiation

8.1 APPLIED EXERCISE: MORAL DILEMMA

This exercise is based on Kohlberg's work on moral judgment.

The Moral Dilemma

A husband is told that his wife needs a special kind of drug if she is to survive a severe illness. The medication is extremely expensive, and the husband can raise only half the needed funds. When he begs the inventor of the drug for a reduced price, he is rebuffed because the inventor wants to make back the money for research and development of the drug and feels he deserves a profit from the medicine's sale. The husband then considers stealing the medicine.

Is it morally justified to steal the medicine?

8.2 APPLIED EXERCISE: JUST VOICE/CARING VOICE DILEMMA

This exercise is based on one of Gilligan's workshops.

The Moral Dilemma

A husband has been working for a corporation for over 10 years and is finally being considered for an important upper-management position. This company expects its management team to always be ready to respond to important business needs. This means subcontracting the family (whenever there is a need for him to travel, there must be a supportive spouse at home who can facilitate his schedule). If he gets this position, the family will be financially secure. However, if he does not get the position (and there is another colleague competing for the position), he would need to leave the company and begin all over again in another company.

There is a lunch set up for the final interview with the two candidates and their wives. If the wife does not attend it would appear there is not the support that is expected. So, attendance at this lunch is critical.

At the same time as this lunch, the wife's very dear friend, who is battling an extremely aggressive cancer, is scheduled for an experimental treatment. This treatment is difficult and cannot be postponed. The friend is terrified and begged her closest friend to accompany her.

Females: Do you go to lunch with your husband or go to the hospital with your friend?

Males: Do you tell your wife to come to lunch with you or do you tell her to go to the hospital with her friend and you will find another job and begin again?

8.3 APPLIED EXERCISE: SELF-ASSESSMENT OF EQ SKILLS

Emotional intelligence (EQ) is the ability to be aware of yourself, understand yourself, and be aware of how to manage relationships. Keep in mind that these competencies are the psychological muscle that enables people to move from being passive receivers of their moral code to becoming active producers of their moral code. These questions are aimed at helping you assess your strengths and weaknesses when it comes to your emotional intelligence. Remember these skills can be learned and, therefore, can be taught (hint: useful to think of parenting when you are going through this exercise).

Rate the following statements as
(0) NEVER / (1) SOMETIMES / (2) OFTEN / (3) ALWAYS

Emotional and Self-awareness Domain

- I am clear about my feelings that translate my emotions.
- Emotions are an important part of my daily life.
- My mood affects the way I conduct my day.
- My mood affects those around me.
- It is easy to put my feelings into words.
- I tell others my true feelings.
- I find it easy to describe my feelings.
- I know my values and their priority in my life.
- I know when I'm going to be angry.
- I can be objective about my thoughts and feelings.

Emotional and Self-management Domain

- I accept responsibility for my reactions.
- I find it easy to make goals and stick with them.
- I am emotionally balanced.
- I am a patient person.
- I can accept criticism without becoming angry.
- I can handle stress well.
- Only those issues that affect me directly bother me.
- I can control my anger.
- I control urges to overindulge in things damaging to me.
- I direct my energies to creative work.

Social-awareness Domain

- I think about the impact of my decisions on others.
- I can tell when people around me are becoming annoyed.
- I can sense others' mood changes.
- I am supportive when giving bad news to others.
- I generally understand the way others feel.
- It bothers me when others suffer.
- I know when to speak and when to be silent.
- I care about others.
- I am politically aware.
- My friends can tell me intimate things about themselves.

Relationships and Social-skills Domain

- I am able to show affection to those I care about.
- I can share my deep feelings with others.
- I can motivate others.
- I am an optimistic person.
- I make friends easily and can build bonds easily.
- I am described as sociable and fun.
- I like helping others.
- I can calm someone down if they are upset.
- I am a team player.
- I am considered a leader.

Assess your **strong areas** (strongest domain)—add up the (2) OFTEN / (3) ALWAYS ratings.

Assess your **areas that require strengthening** (weakness domain)—add up the (0) NEVER / (1) SOMETIMES ratings.

- Using your strongest domain, give an example of how you demonstrate your strength in daily life.
- Review your weakest domain; give an example of how this affects you and others in your daily life.
- What steps can you take to strengthen yourself in your weak areas? How will this benefit you?

NOTES

1. 1898/1980—Piaget, J., and B. Inhelder. (1969). *The Psychology of the Child*. New York: Basic Books.
2. Kohlberg, L., and C. Gilligan. (1971). "The Adolescent as a Philosopher: The Discovery of the Self in the Post-conventional World." *Daedalus*, 100, 1051–1086.
3. Gilligan, C. (1982). *In a Different Voice: Psychological Theory and Women's Development*. Cambridge, MA: Harvard University Press.
4. Goleman, Daniel. (1995). *Emotional Intelligence*. New York: Bantam Books.
5. This chart is based on the work of Daniel Goleman. (1995). *Emotional Intelligence*. New York: Bantam Books.

UNIT THREE

EMPATHY AND DEVELOPING NEGOTIATION SKILLS

CHAPTER 9

UNDERSTANDING OUR CHARACTER TRAITS AND HOW OTHERS SEE US

WHY SHOULD WE UNDERSTAND OUR CHARACTER TRAITS? WHY IS IT IMPORTANT TO KNOW HOW OTHERS SEE US?

Knowing our strong personal character traits enables us to perform different interpersonal tasks successfully. This is part of the compelling journey into yourself. This text has emphasized awareness of values, goals, important norms (rules), moral code, moral judgment, and emotional intelligence. In this process of developing the critical competencies for negotiation and managing conflicts, it is important to honor your past, specifically the way you have navigated your relationships. This leads to personal growth because you become conscious of your strengths so you can own them. When you are open to how life has shaped you, then you can let life become your teacher.

Assessing yourself and reflecting on how you reached this point allows for integration. Integration is a vital way of returning to yourself. The act of reflection helps review experiences and gives new meaning to life. When we take time to reflect, we see our past characteristics in new ways, and appreciate and honor who we have been as well as who we have become. We see with greater clarity the pattern of our lives that gives us uniqueness, or special identity. These very patterns—based on our values, goals, moral code, and character—foster new development and learning. We become comforted by our reflections, because by remembering our past achievements, we come to be at peace with the present. We cannot help being awed when facing ourselves.

Those with strong supportive life experiences can continue to build on those strengths. Those with difficult histories can celebrate the strength gained from surviving those adversities. Our past accompanies us in memories, experiences, and accomplishments as well as in our daily habits. In order to build a future congruent with our goals (dreams) and aspirations, we need to revisit our past and look clearly at our present. By living in both realms, we gain an enhanced vision: one that opens all possibilities, and one that helps us choose the negotiating skills we want to master. Drawing on past accomplishments truly prepares you to build a future filled with confidence.

Two American psychologists, Joseph Luft (1916–2014) and Harrington (Harry) Ingham (1914–1995), created the Johari Window in 1955[1]; the word "Johari" is derived from their first names. The Johari Window focused on people understanding themselves as well as others in a give-and-take process. The window has four areas or quadrants; this heuristic exercise enables you to become aware of:

- Your open quadrant, which is the part of self that is disclosed to others. Sharing this part of self can help to build trust with colleagues and group members. This open area represents the traits that your peers are aware of. This includes your thoughts, dreams, goals, feelings, behaviors, knowledge, skills, attitudes, and public history. Try to avoid over-sharing in your self-disclosure to others. Avoid disclosing personal information, which could damage people's respect for you.
- The hidden quadrant represents the part of self that holds information that peers are unaware of. These are things you know about yourself, but that others do not know. This quadrant can be reduced by recognizing trusting relationships and by encouraging healthy self-disclosure.
- The blind area represents traits that you have not selected, but your peers have chosen. Actually, this can be considered your blind spot, information you do not know about yourself. Feedback from this area helps you learn things about yourself that others see, but you cannot. This is important for personal growth. By getting feedback from others, your blind area will shrink and your open area will grow. Also, be sensitive if you find personal feedback offensive.
- The unknown quadrant represents things that are unknown by you and others. This area reflects the behaviors or motivations that are not recognized by anyone. There is a collective ignorance of the existence of these character traits.

This communication model is only one way is to examine and appreciate our identity character traits. I chose it for this chapter because it is used successfully in corporate settings and in self-help groups. This is also used in therapy. For example, one therapeutic objective is to enlarge the open area while reducing the blind area and the unknown area. This would result in a greater knowledge of oneself. Additionally, one could voluntarily disclose some of the hidden area in order to gain greater intimacy and friendship. Keep in mind, life is a work in progress. To get value from this self-awareness exercise, take some quiet time to reflect on both the changes and constants in your life. Trace the origins of your successes, particularly in your most successful relationships. Discover your creative potential for ensuring connected trusting relationships in your life. Reflect on the self-appreciation exercise in Chapter 7 of this text. This exercise will define your lenses of how you see the world. What are our filters that have been created by our life experiences? This exercise will set the stage for a further exploration of our needs, concerns, and expectations about our future relationships (personal and professional).

9.1 APPLIED EXERCISE: SELF-AWARENESS

Johari Window, graphic model of interpersonal awareness[2]

	Known by Self (me)	**Unknown** by Self (me)
Known by Others	open Self known by Self (me) known by Others	blind Self unknown by Self (me) known by Others
Unknown by Others	hidden Self known by Self (me) unknown by Others	XXX unknown by Self (me) unknown by Others

Fig. 9.1 Johari Window

- Describe your open self.
- What parts of your self are hidden (are there parts of yourself that you cannot or will not share)?

9.2 APPLIED EXERCISE: ASSESS YOUR PERSONAL TRAITS/CHARACTERISTICS[3]

Everyone has certain personal traits/characteristics that make us unique and enable us to perform different tasks successfully. Reflect on the list of traits and circle all you feel best describe you. Then select eight traits that you have clear evidence of in your life experience.

Adaptable	Efficient	Independent	Physically fit
Analytical	Emotional	Inquisitive	Practical
Accurate	Empathetic	Intelligent	Productive
Adventurous	Enterprising	Interesting	Rational
Artistic	Entrepreneurial	Kind	Respectful
Assertive	Energetic	Leader	Responsible
Accommodating	Entertaining	Levelheaded	Responsive
Challenging	Enthusiastic	Loyal	Self-assured
Civic-minded	Expressive	Listener	Self-controlled
Committed	Friendly	Negotiator	Self-motivated
Communicates well	Fun	Nurturer	Self-starter
Compassionate	Fashionable	Organizer	Sense of humor
Confidant	Good attitude	Observer	Sensitive
Creative	Hardworking	Open-minded	Social
Curious	High standards	Original	Spiritual
Collaborative	Imaginative	People-oriented	Stable
Coordinated	Influential	Perfectionist	Tolerant
Decision-making	Innovative	Personable	Trustworthy
Dedicated	Inspiring	Persuasive	Other:
Dependable	Intuitive	Problem solver	

Of the eight you selected, now choose four as your most prominent traits. Place a check next to those four. Consider the self and how you present yourself in everyday life. Think about your open and hidden parts of self.

Choose one or more significant others in your network to confirm your personal traits/characteristics. Try to include a work colleague, a friend, and a relative (choose people who know you well). Do not share your results from your personal assessment exercise. This exercise is aimed at understanding the personality characteristics or traits that make each one of us unique and enhance our ability to manage conflicts. The blind part of the self will be discovered after your significant other(s) completes your characteristic profile. Copy the list below and have the other person circle all the traits/characteristics that apply to you.

9.3 APPLIED EXERCISE: CONFIRMING PERSONAL TRAITS/CHARACTERISTICS[4]

Duplicate this page and have a work colleague, a friend, and a relative select the traits they see in you. Be sure to choose people who know you and whose opinions you respect.

Adaptable	Efficient	Independent	Physically fit
Analytical	Emotional	Inquisitive	Practical
Accurate	Empathetic	Intelligent	Productive
Adventurous	Enterprising	Interesting	Rational
Artistic	Entrepreneurial	Kind	Respectful
Assertive	Energetic	Leader	Responsible
Accommodating	Entertaining	Levelheaded	Responsive
Challenging	Enthusiastic	Loyal	Self-assured
Civic-minded	Expressive	Listener	Self-controlled
Committed	Friendly	Negotiator	Self-motivated
Communicates well	Fun	Nurturer	Self-starter
Compassionate	Fashionable	Organizer	Sense of humor
Confidant	Good attitude	Observer	Sensitive
Creative	Hardworking	Open-minded	Social
Curious	High standards	Original	Spiritual
Collaborative	Imaginative	People-oriented	Stable
Coordinated	Influential	Perfectionist	Tolerant
Decision-making	Innovative	Personable	Trustworthy
Dedicated	Inspiring	Persuasive	Other:
Dependable	Intuitive	Problem solver	

Consider the self and how others see you in everyday life.

1. Before your significant other completes your personality traits/characteristics as they view them, comment on how you think this person will describe your traits.
2. After your significant other completes your personality traits/characteristics as they view them, comment on how you feel about this person's description of your traits.
3. Compare your expectations with the results from your significant other. Keep in mind that you are focusing on the open area and the blind area (your blind spot). What do you feel about the comparison? Does this feedback from others help you learn about yourself?

Note: The blind area of the self will be discovered after your significant others complete your characteristic profile.

9.4 APPLIED EXERCISE: IDENTIFY THE SKILLS YOU HAVE LEARNED OR DEVELOPED

Use this list of skills and select those that are supported by your experience, education, technical training, on-the-job training, or achievement. Keep in mind that skills relate to knowledge and information you need on the job. Personal characteristics are the traits that make you successful.

Go through this list four times:

1.   CHECK all skills that apply
2.   CIRCLE those skills you enjoy doing (whether you do them well or not)*
3.   UNDERLINE those skills you believe you do well
4.   HIGHLIGHT those skills that the "market is buying"

Communicating

Communicating verbally	Negotiating
Compromising	Persuading
Enforcing regulations	Presenting ideas
Interviewing	Performing
Fund-raising	Speaking publicly
Lecturing	Relating to customers
Listening	Resolving issues
Managing conflict	Selling
Mediating	

Others: _____

Teaching/Helping Others

Caring for	Interpreting
Counseling	Intuition
Giving directions	Recommending/prescribing
Identifying	Rehabilitating
Improving	

Others: _____

Developing People

Advising	Developing
Assessing performances	Motivating
Coaching	Team-building
Consulting	Training
Counseling	Teaching

Others: _____

Managing/Directing

Advising	Interpreting policy
Approving	Managing change
Decision-making	Managing people
Delegating	Problem-solving
Developing procedures	Project-managing
Directing	Restructuring
Implementing	Setting standards
Instructing	

Others: _____

Ideas/Information

Conceptualizing	Managing details
Corresponding	Proposals of grants
Creating	Recording
Designing	Scripting
Drafting	Translating
Editing	Writing
Illustrating	

Others: _____

Research/Analysis

Analyzing	Judging
Compiling	Measuring
Evaluating	Observing
Following up	Projecting
Gathering data	Researching
Interpreting	Reviewing

Others: _____

Systems

Clarifying	Inventory
Computing	Organizing
Data analysis	Planning
Designing	Programming
Developing procedures	Retrieving
Engineering	Storing
Formulating	

Others: _____

Financial

Auditing	Cost accounting
Bookkeeping	General accounting
Budgeting	Payroll
Controlling	

Others: _____

*Note: To identify the skills you enjoy, keep a daily diary to note down when you have been doing something for three hours but you feel that only 15 or 20 minutes have passed. Another notable moment might be when, at the end of a long day, you realize you feel tired but would still define your day as wonderful. What were you engaged in doing that day to make you feel happy and satisfied?

9.5 APPLIED EXERCISE: IDENTIFY STRENGTHS AND DEVELOP A SKILLS-BASED PLAN FOR YOUR CAREER DECISIONS

Your STRENGTHS: List the skills that are checked, circled, underlined, and highlighted from applied exercise 9.4. The skills that you selected all four times are your strengths:

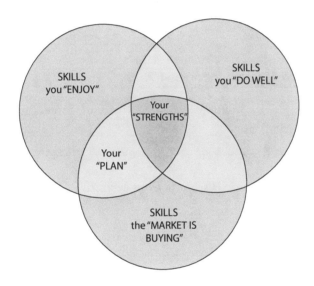

Your SKILLS-BASED PLAN: Focus on the skills that you enjoy and that the market is buying (those skills that you selected three times, the skills that are checked, circled, and highlighted). List these skills that you enjoy doing and that the market is buying, but that you need to learn how to master. Your career plan should include education, training, and on-the-job experience that will help develop these skills (see applied exercise 9.4).

9.6 APPLIED EXERCISE: WRITE A "POSITION STATEMENT" WITH YOUR BRIEF BACKGROUND, SKILLS/STRENGTHS, AND PERSONAL TRAITS/CHARACTERISTICS

Now, you are going to answer the "Tell Me About Yourself" section. This is going to be your opening statement to introduce your background, skills/strengths, and personal character traits. Whether you are being interviewed for a job, graduate schools, internship, or scholarship, this is an important and helpful way to begin the conversation. The aim is to be brief, clear, and informative. Following this structure will help relax you and help put the other parties involved at ease, plus it can even serve as a wonderful ice breaker during a tense situation.

When you have written out your statement, read it out loud several times and memorize it. Find a friend or family member to time you—try not to let this statement take more than 75 seconds to say. Be sure to read or recite the statement slowly and deliberately. Pause at every period (take a full breath, inhale and exhale) and pause at every comma (take a half breath, inhale *or* exhale).

Position Statement: "Tell Me About Yourself"

"My name is _____ with ___ years in the work force. I have a/an (major/minor/specialization/concentration) in _____
_____.

My demonstrated strengths include (*list those from exercise 9.5*):
- Example
- Example
- Example
- Example
- Example
- Example

My personal traits/characteristics are (*list those from exercise 9.3*):
- Example
- Example
- Example
- Example
- Example
- Example

Example: Defining Yourself as a Professional, or Professional Self-awareness

"Over five years of increasingly responsible experience in the work force. I am a Behavior Science major with a specialization in Health Care Management and a concentration in Managing Conflict. My demonstrated strengths include:

- Communicating
- Analyzing
- Observing
- Problem-solving
- Planning
- Implementing

The takeaway: I am a responsible and dependable critical thinker who is empathetic, civic-minded, organized, and works well under pressure."

Note: Use bullets—they are easier for HR (or hiring people) to read and remember. Do not write a paragraph.

CHAPTER 10

STEREOTYPING AND OUR WORLDVIEW

By Chelsea Kuo, Ph.D., Sociology

DO STEREOTYPES AFFECT HOW WE SEE OTHERS AND OURSELVES?

STEREOTYPING AND THE CREATION OF A WORLDVIEW

Although very few people think of themselves as holding stereotypes or prejudices, much less as being discriminatory in a racist or sexist way, we often hear such remarks as "I am not prejudiced, but...", "I am not a sexist (or a racist), but...", "Not that I am stereotyping, but...."

We all believe that stereotypes, prejudice, and discrimination are negative and harmful. These concepts are inevitable in all societies, however, and at the same time hard to discover.

STEREOTYPES MAKE SENSE

We must begin by remembering that we make sense of the world by meaning making and by attaching these meanings to the objects of our perceptions. We then find it easy and efficient to group our perceptions into categories, which is the first step toward stereotyping. Symbolic interactionism teaches us that we understand the social world we live in through cultural symbols. It is through our interactions with one another that we create a shared understanding of reality. The fact that all human communications take place through the perception and interpretation of symbols means that we do not respond directly to reality but to the meanings we attach to the real world. Thus, although stereotyping has many negative consequences, it must be understood to be part of an inevitable quest for understanding that is natural to humans. Indeed, because it makes sense.

STEREOTYPES CAN BE POSITIVE OR NEGATIVE

A stereotype can be defined as a belief that links a group with a specific set of characteristics. We are stereotyping whenever we associate certain groups with certain traits or characteristics, inferring the group members' traits and abilities from these individuals' looks and behaviors. Most basically, a stereotype is the picture that comes into your mind when you are thinking of a particular group. Stereotypes are transmitted through socialization, via such agents as media discourse and everyday conversations engaged in at home and school and in the workplace.

There are positive stereotypes, such as "Asians are good at math" and "women are detail-oriented." Also stereotypes can be statistically true, as in, "men generally are taller than women," "women tend to sacrifice career for family," and "Asian Americans perform well on the SAT's math sections." What such stereotypes fail to account for, however, is the deeper rationale beneath the supposed reality.

STEREOTYPES CAN GIVE RISE TO PREJUDICE AND DISCRIMINATION

If stereotypes can be both positive and statistically true, are they really as bad as we are always being told they are? The answer is yes. Stereotypes influence how we perceive a particular group of people, process information about the group, and respond to and interact with its members. Therefore, stereotypes directed toward a group can easily elicit prejudice, and individually held prejudices can lead to hurtful actions. In short, discrimination begins with stereotyping.

In summary of the macroscopic view, although stereotypes are sometimes positive or statistically true, it always comes with negative connotations and consequences. However, since stereotypes are a natural byproduct of how people make sense of the world, getting rid of stereotypes requires constant effort. This demystification of stereotypes doesn't come naturally, and that's exactly why studying disciplines such as sociology and conflict resolution can lead the fight in this regard.

STEREOTYPING AND ITS RELATION TO OUR INTROSPECTIVE JOURNEY

Now, let us focus on the microscopic aspects of stereotyping. Beginning with our perceptions of how others see us, we create an image that influences our self-concept (see chapters 2 and 4 for discussions on G.H. Mead and C.H. Cooley). Our self-concept influences our behavior. Our behavior, in turn, influences the actions of others toward us. These actions influence our perception of how others see us; hence we are back at the starting point. As a teacher, I can affect the self-concepts of my students by the nature of the communication I direct toward them.

How I perceive the communication I receive from my students influences my self-concept as an instructor. Thus, my subsequent communication will reflect that assessment.

The notion of the looking-glass self was first introduced in 1902 by Charles Horton Cooley, who suggested that we see ourselves in the position of other people and then in our mind's eye. We view ourselves as we imagine they see us.[1] George Herbert Mead added to Cooley's work with his theory of mind, self, and society.[2] Harry Stack Sullivan coined the term "reflected appraisal" to describe that we develop an image of ourselves from the way we think others view us.[3] Basically, what we are saying is that how we think others see us affects our self-concept. In short, this cycle illustrates the chicken-and-egg nature of the self-concept, which is shaped by significant others in the past, helps to govern our present behavior, and influences the way others view us. So, to create a view of ourselves (and of those around us), we tend to use categories of others. These people categories or stereotypes include gender, ethnic groups, and cultural groups.

10.1 APPLIED EXERCISE: GENDER STEREOTYPING

What does it mean to be masculine or feminine in our society? The family introduces the child to the definitions, meanings, stereotypes, and values of gender to the child. The majority of males and females embody these definitions, meanings, and stereotypes that then get reinforced by school, friends, work, and social media, thus perpetuating existing social/cultural views of gender.

1. Divide the class into groups of males and females.
2. Each group will make a list of adjectives that describe the gender stereotype.
3. The males will ask themselves how they think *women see men.*
4. The females will ask themselves how they think *men see women.*
5. Each group selects the ten top descriptive adjectives and lists them in rank order.
6. Have the groups come together and compare and contrast their lists with rationales.

Debrief

This becomes very lively when each group corrects the other's stereotypes.

Note: This stereotyping exercise can be done with any groups. There was successful understanding when this was done with:

faculty and students
staff and supervisors
veteran students and traditional college students

NOTES

1. Cooley, C.H. (1902). *Human Nature and Social Order*. New York: Scriber's.
2. Mead, G.H. (1971). "Mind, Self, and Society." In M. Truzzi (Ed.), *Sociology: The Classic Statements*. New York: Random House.
3. Sullivan, H.S. (1953). *The Interpersonal Theory of Psychiatry*. New York: Norton.

CHAPTER 11

UNDERSTANDING ACTIVE LISTENING

WHAT ARE THE COMPONENTS OF COMMUNICATION? WHY IS IT
IMPORTANT TO BE A GOOD LISTENER?

A two-way conversation contains four different messages:

Fig. 11.1: John and Martha

Copyright © Depositphotos/
Wavebreakmedia.

John intends to say this and *thinks* he did.

Martha intends to say this and *thinks* she did.

But Martha hears it this way.

But John is sure he heard this.

Active Listening: learn to listen and listen to learn.

Communication starts with listening: active listening leads to successful negotiation.

"I know that you believe you understand what you think I said, but I am not sure you realize that what you heard is not what I meant!"

Essential ingredients of successful communication (sharing information) include:

***Speaker* (*sender*)**: the person who originates the communication

***Listener* (*receiver*)**: the person to whom the message is directed

Message (encoded and decoded): the statement or question the speaker expresses

***Feedback* (*verbal or nonverbal reaction*)**: the listener's response or reaction to the message

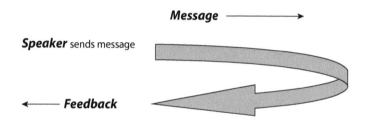

Message ⟶

Speaker sends message

⟵ **Feedback**

Listener receives the ***message*** and gives ***feedback*** to the ***speaker***. **Feedback** can be verbal or nonverbal.

Fig. 11.6 Active Listening

Everyone can improve the capacity to listen and it is well worth the effort. Active listening is at the heart of intimacy and connection. When we are able to listen to another person with attention and care, that person feels validated, respected, and enhanced. Actually, when we enhance the other person, we enhance the self. The following are the components of good listening:

- **Hear the message**. Listen to both the verbal and nonverbal information.
- **Interpret the message**. A good interpretation is a match-up of meaning between speaker and listener.
- **Evaluate the message**. The listener's opinion should be based on all available information. Ask questions.
- **Respond to the message**. Good listening means giving the speaker an appropriate response, verbally and/or nonverbally.

Now let's define the purpose for listening by:

- Focusing on the important parts of the message
- Investing the energy needed to listen effectively
- Knowing why you are listening; it helps you focus your listening energy

Keep in mind that it is important to know your purpose because it keeps you focused on the key element of the message. Also, at this point try to remember that you can't change the other person. This is a time to learn, inquire, and acknowledge. At this point, there is a sharing of perceptions and feelings, not attributions or judgments.

In order to let the other person know that you are listening, you must attend to the message by:

- Making eye contact with the speaker
- Adjusting your body posture
- Providing verbal and nonverbal acknowledgment
- Clearing your mind of other thoughts
- Avoiding distracting behaviors that keep you from listening to the speaker

We have already discussed how important it is to trust.[1] The other person must be appreciated by us, which means we must respect them and their right to talk.

Effective negotiation needs successful communication. Successful communication depends on our ability to listen. We take listening very much for granted—our own as well as that of others. Paying attention to what someone is telling us is routine and it strikes us as almost instinctive, like breathing. Listening is merely a tool for collecting a speaker's information and understanding the meaning. However, we listen by choice. When we are listening we're thinking. We decide whether we will listen, when, and to what (or whom). Listening is an active process in which we:

- take in information
- interpret it
- evaluate it
- prioritize it

Listening is more of an art than a craft. To effectively communicate, we need to demonstrate the ability to listen proactively. A good listener brings to the conversations a deliberate strategy, a design that keeps the speaker ever alert to the meaning and nuance of their message.

There are very different perceptions of what it is to be a listener. To paraphrase John F. Kennedy's speech given at Amherst College, MA, on October 26, 1963, in praise of the poet, Robert Frost, on the nature of art: "If listening is to fulfill its true mission, society must set the listener free to connect." We must never forget that listening is not a form of solitude; it is a form of engagement.

Proactive listening is a form of engagement. Proactive listeners create action, instead of merely following it. We are talking about *conversational relatedness* that must become the basis of this mode of listening. The very feeling of marginality must give way to conversational relatedness if this perception is to be the content and basis of successful listening. *Listening* is something we know in the abstract and from a distance. It is only when we—or someone close to us—personally experiences the benefits of being listened to that it bears in on us with immediate impact and somehow it becomes real. Therefore, we must learn to listen and listen to learn. It is important to consider the listener's rational and emotional landscape, and that includes ego, respect, and trust.

Listening reflects the art of being fully present without judgment or distraction. When we are fully present, we are not thinking about our work or worrying about how we are coming across. Our mind is free from judging our self or the other. While listening, we are not formulating our responses or considering how we might best present our issue. Our thoughts are not stuck in the past or wandering to the future. We are not doodling, daydreaming, or playing with our phones. We are fully open and receptive to what the other person is saying without having to change, fix, correct, or advise. We are there with that person and nowhere else.

These are some suggested listening qualities: **P-R-E-S-E-N-T**

- **Proactive participation** in the conversations; forge strong partnerships with conversational partners
- Systematically **Review** incoming information
- **Empathy**; understand another's feelings
- **Sidestep** occasional negative or belittling remarks by weighing in with questioning or other forms of response
- Make a conscious **Effort** to pay attention—stay focused and respond accordingly
- **Neutralize** snap judgments in order to get the full story in order to make an objective assessment
- **Tenaciously track** both the speaker and the message in order to get the substance and mood

When you are actively listening, you are present (P-R-E-S-E-N-T) in the conversation. We listen best when we are relaxed, centered, and have a sense of inner peace and well-being. So, we could say that the art of actively listening to another person is linked to the act of quieting and centering the self. Active listening is an important challenge for everyone.

There will be many times when we can't listen in this open way. Other people will have to make do with our partial attention if we are stressed, tense, preoccupied, or in the throes of a strong emotional episode. We do not listen well when our mind is already made up and we have our own agenda. At this point, we are merely waiting for the other person to finish speaking so we can make our point, rather than paying attention. Managing conflict would take a big leap forward if our wish to listen and understand the other were as great as our wish to be listened to and understood.

On the other hand, *hearing* is a passive process that is a solitary, isolated, individual act. We hear by chance because something in our immediate environment stimulates the ears. Hearing has little to do with understanding.

Hearing versus Listening

Hearing (passive)---**Listening** (active)

- Hearing is an involuntary action. We can hear without choosing to listen.
- Hearing is the special sense in which noises and tones are received as stimuli.
- Hearing is a sensory experience that gathers sound waves indiscriminately.

- Listening is a voluntary action.
- Listening includes more than sounds received by the ear and transmitted to the brain.
- Listening includes interpreting or processing that sound that is received.
- Listening is a key to successful communication.

11.1 APPLIED EXERCISE: HOW TO PREPARE FOR A DIFFICULT/COURAGEOUS CONVERSATION

Identify a meaningful/difficult/courageous conversation.

1. Identify the parties with their different stories.
2. Identify the kind of conversation using the chart below.

Identify different conversations

- **What is your purpose?**—remember, you can't change it
- **Learn**—remember: inquire and acknowledge
- **Expression**—remember: share perceptions and feelings, not attributions or judgments
- **Problem-solving**—how might you manage conflicts?

Table 11.1: Difficult/Courageous Conversations*

INFORMATIONAL CONVERSATION	IDENTITY CONVERSATION	EMOTIONAL CONVERSATION
A "What Happened?" Conversation	Our identity is connected to our feelings	A "Feelings" Conversation (Feelings—way we translate emotions)
Get curious about each other's story Explore their story: Learn to listen, listen to learn Share your story: Do not blame – "when you do X, I feel..." Disentangle INTENT from IMPACT: Your/their intentions Unintended impacts Abandon blame: Your contribution to blame Their contribution to blame How may each of you change your contributions in the future	Have I balanced my self-image to include the good and the bad? What might I be denying? What might I be exaggerating? What about this conversation hooks me? Have I prepared for their response?	Explore your feelings: What is my predominant feeling? What other feelings am I having? Prepare to share your feelings: How can I communicate these feelings? Consider their feelings: Reflect on my feelings as it relates to their story. What might they be feeling? Why?

*For an illustration of a difficult/courageous conversation, read my impact statement, which I read in court, found in the Epilogue.

11.2 APPLIED EXERCISE: RANKING COMMON REASONS FOR NOT LISTENING

Table 11.2: Some Common Reasons For Not Listening

RANK 1=LEAST 10=MOST	WHAT YOU SAY TO YOURSELF	HOW OFTEN YOU SAY IT: NEVER/ SOMETIMES/ALWAYS
	I didn't like my partner.	
	I didn't want to believe what I knew you were about to tell me.	
	I don't like the way my partner talked.	
1	I wanted to talk first.	
	I was not interested in the subject.	
3	I was thinking about what I was going to say.	
4	I was too upset or worried about other things.	
	I'd rather daydream or doodle.	
	I'd rather give my attention to people or activities around me.	
2	It was too hard to understand.	

11.3 APPLIED EXERCISE: ACTIVE LISTENING/NON-LISTENING (A)

Select groups of three and separate them for confidential instructions:

- Person *A* becomes the speaker, who will tell a three- to five-minute story about something he or she is passionate about. This person is seated during the exercise.
- Person *B* becomes the listener and is seated across from the speaker during the exercise. This person will:
- not interrupt the story, but will ignore the speaker with nonverbal gestures, body language, and facial expressions
- summarize what is remembered about the story without notes
- Person *C* becomes the observer and stands behind the speaker. Person *C* will note how the listener and speaker respond. This person is standing during the exercise.

Instruct the speaker *A* to pick a story that they feel strongly about and to make sure that it takes three to five minutes to tell the entire story: its beginning, middle, and end.

Instruct the listener *B* to listen attentively at the beginning of the story, using eye contact and appropriate body language; then, the listener *B* is to look away, begin playing with their phone, doodling, fidgeting, etc.

Instruct the observer *C* to observe any changes in the speaker *A* and the listener *B*. The observer is standing behind the speaker so that the speaker isn't tempted to tell their story to the observer when the listener appears to stop listening. *C* is to observe the exchange, noting the nonverbal communication and if there is any difference when the listener begins giving cues of indifference. Note if *B*'s listening skills changed when the non-listening gestures are perceived.

Debrief

The listener
- summarizes the highlights of the story
- explains what it felt like ignoring the speaker

The speaker
- explains how it felt telling the story during the exercise
- describes the feeling of telling an emotional story to someone who's not listening

The observer
- describes the initial part of the storytelling
- describes the reactions of the speaker and listener as things begin to change

11.4 APPLIED EXERCISE: ACTIVE LISTENING (B)

Select groups of three and separate them for confidential instructions:

- Person *A* becomes the speaker, who will tell a three- to five-minute story about something he or she is passionate about. This person is seated during the exercise.
- Person *B* becomes the listener and is seated across from the speaker during the exercise. This person will:
- not interrupt the story
- listen intently
- remember the highlights and summarize the story without notes
- report summary of the story to *A*
- Person *C* becomes the observer and stands behind the speaker. Person *C* will note how the listener and speaker respond. This person is standing during the exercise.

Instruct the speaker *A* to pick a story that they feel strongly about and to make sure that it takes three to five minutes to tell the entire story: its beginning, middle, and end.

Instruct the listener *B* to listen attentively at the beginning of the story, using eye contact and appropriate body language; then, the listener *B* is to look away, begin playing with their phone, doodling, fidgeting, etc. *A* must be satisfied that *B* covered all major points as well as have some understanding of the emotional state of *A*.

Instruct the observer *C* to observe the speaker *A* and the listener *B*. The observer is standing behind the speaker so that the speaker isn't tempted to tell their story to the observer. *C* is to observe the exchange, noting the nonverbal communication.

Debrief

The listener
- summarizes the highlights of the story (what was added and/or deleted); did the listener understand and report on the emotional state?

The speaker
- explains how it felt telling the story during the exercise
- describes the feeling of telling an emotional story to someone who's not listening

The observer
- describes the storytelling
- describes the nonverbal reactions of the speaker and listener
- describes the exchange during the summary

11.5 APPLIED EXERCISE: LEARN TO LISTEN AND LISTEN TO LEARN

Table 11.3: Some Perfectly Good Reasons to Become a Better Listener

To learn something.	To show you care.
To be entertained.	To satisfy curiosity.
To understand a situation.	To be safe.
To get information.	To be a good lover.
To be courteous.	To prevent waste.
To be responsible.	To make money.
To prevent accidents.	To avoid embarrassment.
To ask intelligent questions.	To stay out of trouble.
To be a team player.	To save time.
To improve confidence.	To be a discriminating consumer.
To protect your freedom.	To be a supportive friend.
To find out people's needs.	To give an appropriate response.
To reach productivity quota.	To enjoy the sounds of nature.
To be valued and trusted.	To create win-win situations.
To use money more wisely.	To control distractions.
To be more efficient.	To increase concentration.
To make accurate evaluations.	To improve your vocabulary.
To make comparisons.	To build rapport.
To understand and be understood.	To be a better family member.
To analyze the speaker's purpose.	To settle arguments.
To get the best value.	To maintain a flexible attitude.
To improve discipline.	To improve your personality.
To enhance relationships.	To solve problems.
To use the gift of hearing.	To be prepared for sudden shifts in a speaker's topic or intention.
To develop the reputation of being a good listener.	

11.6 APPLIED EXERCISE: ACTIVE LISTENING STATEMENTS AND QUESTIONS

(Examples shared by NYS Mediators)

- **Acknowledging:** "It seems that you are very angry right now. What's the cause?
- **Clarifying:** "Where did you say this happened?
- **Empathizing:** "This must have been very difficult for you."
- **Encouraging:** "Would you mind telling us more?"
- **Normalizing:** "Many people would have felt the same under this circumstance."
- **Open:** Who, What, Where, When, How, etc. questions.
- **Reframing:** "I understand that you feel disappointed when…"
- **Responding:** "You see this situation this way. How do you think others see it?"
- **Soliciting:** "What do you think should happen in this case?"
- **Summarizing:** "If I understood you correctly, you said…. Is this the case?"
- **Validating:** "We appreciate your candor and willingness to…"

Note: Active listening interventions allow disputants an opportunity to continue addressing their concerns, knowing that they are being heard. On the contrary, reactive interventions prevent further communication.

Other examples:

- What is most important to you about this matter?
- What part of this matter are you willing to let go of?
- What would it take for you to make this happen?
- If that didn't work, what else could you do to make this happen?
- How do you feel about this matter?
- How do you think the other person involved in this matter feels?
- What do you need to make yourself feel better?
- What do you think the other person needs?
- What can you say or do to move forward in this matter?
- What is preventing you from saying or doing so?

NOTE

1. See APPLIED EXERCISE 6.1 Trust walk. If we do not trust, we generally will not listen. We have also learned that we need to have self-worth and feel we are deserving of respect (see the chapter on the feelings wheel).

CHAPTER 12
NONVERBAL COMMUNICATION: BODY LANGUAGE AND PROXEMICS

WHY IS IT IMPORTANT TO UNDERSTAND BODY LANGUAGE?
HOW DOES SPACE IMPACT COMMUNICATION?
HOW DO WE READ FACIAL EXPRESSIONS?

NONVERBAL COMMUNICATION—SILENT LANGUAGE

Psychologists tell us that more than 90% of the emotional impact of a message comes from nonverbal sources. Cultural anthropologists, sociologists, and social psychologists describe the nonverbal portion of any message as extremely important. It is the nonverbal message that contains the relational portion of the message and we tend to believe the nonverbal more. Nonverbal communication can repeat the verbal message (a wave while saying good-bye), substitute for the verbal (a silent wave good-bye), or complement and accent the nonverbal (a finger circling the ear to indicate someone's crazy).

Over fifty years ago an exciting science was uncovered and explored. It was called body language and has since also been named kinesics. Body language analyses and kinesics are based on the behavioral patterns of nonverbal communication. There are even clinical studies that reveal the extent to which body language can actually contradict verbal communication. A classic example is the young woman who told her psychiatrist that she was in love with her boyfriend while shaking her head from side to side in subconscious denial. Again, that is why we tend to believe the nonverbal more. These signals from the unconscious can be extremely important in reading others. We need to understand that others are reading our body language. Dr. Edward Hess revealed a kinetic signal, the unconscious widening of a pupil when one sees something pleasant (presented at the American College of Medical Hypnotists). This can be very useful in a poker game. When a player sees an opponent's pupils widen, he can be sure that his opponent is holding a good hand. The other player may not be conscious of his ability to read this signal any more than the other person is conscious of telegraphing his lucky cards. Also, advertisers can use this when showing focus groups a commercial they plan to air (especially when considering the expense of ad time during the Super Bowl). While the commercial is being shown, the eyes of the audience/focus group are observed. The marketing people detect when there is any widening of the pupils, which is a subconscious indication of a pleasant response. Another study showed that the pupils of a man's eyes became twice as large when he saw a picture of a beautiful nude woman.

Body language can include any non-reflexive or reflexive movement of a part or all of the body, used to communicate an emotional message to the outside world. To understand this unspoken language, you must also take into consideration cultural and environmental differences. Keep in mind that verbal messages use a single channel—we cannot say two words simultaneously. Nonverbal messages do not arrive in a sequenced manner. We see people's facial expressions, their head and body movements, the way they are dressed, and their gestures. Additionally, verbal messages are discrete; that is, they have a clear beginning and end. Nonverbal messages are continuous and, unlike the spoken word, they are mostly not deliberate. There are just too many nonverbal channels to be able to control all of them. Therefore, how can we know the meaning of the signals we are reading? Verbal and nonverbal messages differ in their degree of ambiguity. In general, nonverbal messages are more ambiguous. The best way to find out is to ask for verbal clarification.

The theory and research with nonverbal communication focuses on the structures and conditions within which communication takes place (the communication environment), the physical characteristics of the communicators, and their behaviors.

Most nonverbal research (but not all) is on appearance and behavior of the person communicating. The body is the message, which is the face, head, and body. When reading body language, the focus is on these aspects:

- gestures
- eye contact
- facial expressions
- vocal behavior
- trunk and shoulders
- arm and wrist
- hand and fingers
- hip
- leg and ankle
- foot and neck
- overall posture
- general presentation of self (including clothing)
- touch
- personal space

It is important to remember there are influential nonverbal cues that are not visible body movements. These include posture, body shape or physique, attractiveness, height, weight, hair, skin color or tone, odors (body or breath), clothes, jewelry, and accessories (such as handbags or attaché cases). Body movement and position generally include gestures, movements of the body (limbs, hands, head, feet, and legs), facial expressions (smiles, frowns), eye behavior (blinking, direction and length of gaze, and pupil dilation), and posture. Positions of the head, shoulders, and brows are considered major areas of nonverbal communication. There are gender similarities and differences.

Another dimension to consider in nonverbal communication is vocal behavior, which deals with *how* something is said; the nonverbal vocal cues surrounding common speech. There are the sound vibrations made with the vocal cords during talk that are a function of changes in pitch, duration, loudness, and silence. In addition, there are the sounds that result from physiological mechanisms other than the vocal cords, like the oral or nasal cavities. There is research on pitch level, duration of sound (clipped or drawn out), pauses, loudness, resonance, rate, rhythm, and intruding sounds ("uh," "um," "ah"). Laughing, belching, yawning, swallowing, moaning may affect the outcome of the interaction. Keep in mind that "it is not the words we say, but the music we play" (Dave Wolffe).

Verbal and nonverbal communication systems operate together. Nonverbal communication functions to express emotions, convey attitudes (like/dislike, dominance/submission, etc.), presenting one's self to the other, accompanying speech for the purpose of emphasis, feedback, managing turn-taking, attention, etc. (my background is Italian—I simply cannot talk without using hand gestures). Furthermore, there is agreement in our culture or subcultures on some signal or gesture, such as "A-OK," "Peace," and "V for Victory."

Make sure you consider the physical environment (store, church/temple, school, playground, club/bar, home, street, etc.) because environments can affect our moods, choices of words, and actions. Other factors that are part of this analysis are furniture, architectural style, interior décor, lighting, colors, temperature, noise, and music. You also form an impression by the so-called traces of activity such as trash, discarded food, and wastepaper. Timing and the perception of time need to be considered because they are clearly a part of understanding nonverbal communication factors. The frequency, tempo, and rhythm of actions definitely impact communication even though they may not be part of the physical environment.

Now to broaden our analysis of nonverbal communication even further, consider the spatial environment. There are studies called proxemics and small-group ecology (ecology is the relationship of an individual to the environment). These researchers are concerned with how people respond to spatial relationships in formal and informal settings. We know that humans have a sense of territory, a need for a shell of territory around them. This ranges from the city dweller with a tight and close shell to the larger bubble of the suburbanite with the yard/open spaces to the country people with wide-open space. The fact is that we all possess zones of territory. We carry these zones with us and we respond in different ways if our space or territory is threatened or breached. Actually, how we guard our zones and how we aggress to other zones is an integral part of how we relate to others. Proxemics is the study of the use and perception of intimate, personal, social, and public space. Anthropologist Edward T. Hall coined the word *proxemics* to describe his theories and observations about zones of territory and how we use them.[1] Hall's proxemics chart of space and social interaction describes:

- his theories and observations about zones of territory and how people use them
- the ways people use space to communicate facts and signals to others; suggestions on how to standardize and classify by measurement

Table 12.1: Hall's Proxemics Chart of Space and Social Interaction

CLOSE DISTANCE	FAR DISTANCE	DISTANCE ZONE
Actual contact	From six to 18 inches	Intimate Distance
1½ feet to 2½ feet	2½ feet to 4 feet	Personal Distance
4 feet to 7 feet	7 feet to 12 feet	Social Distance
20 feet to 25 feet	Over 25 feet	Public Distance

Hall reminds us that distances are arrived at by human interactions and not by measurements. Cultural differences are critical to understand. For example, there is no Japanese word for *privacy*, but this does not mean there is no concept of privacy. To the Japanese, privacy exists in terms of their house/living space. There is no Arabic word for *rape* (rape reflects attitude toward the body).

Intimate and personal distance: Between two women in most U.S. cultures, a close intimate state is acceptable, while in an Arab culture such a state is acceptable between two men. Men will frequently walk hand in hand in many Arab and Mediterranean countries. Think about crowded subway cars, elevators, crowded beaches, clubs/bars, and concerts. When you are at close intimate distance, you are overwhelmingly aware of your partner. Hall points out that this is a way to standardize a baby science and that there are dozens of clarifications necessary. When two people meet in the street, they usually stop at a far personal distance (2½ to 4 feet) from each other in order to chat. At a party, they may tend to move toward the close phase of personal distance. People are making a statement with their distance. A boss uses distance to dominate a seated employee. To the employee, he or she tends to loom above and gain height and strength. The boss is reinforcing "you work for me" without saying it. The big boss will have a big desk to put him or her at a distance.

Social and public space: The close phase is generally the distance at which we transact impersonal business. It is the distance we assume when we meet the client, the new director, or the manager. It is the distance the homeowner (especially female) keeps from the (especially male) repair person, shop clerk, or delivery person. Eye contact in the intimate/personal distance zone should not be constant and direct (unbroken stares can get creepy). However, at the social distance it is not proper to look briefly and then look away. The only contact you have is visual, and so tradition dictates that you hold the person's eyes during conversation. According to Hall, failing to hold the person's eyes is the same as excluding him or her from the conversation.

Public space is the farthest extension of our territorial boundaries. The close phase of public distance is suited for more formal gatherings like a teacher's lecture to students, or a facilitator at a conference. The far phase of public distance is for politicians; actors in the theater; and safety or security, as with dangerous animals. Certain animal species will let you come within only a certain distance before moving away. While on the subject of animal species and distance, there is frequently the danger of misinterpreting the true meaning of territorial zones. For example, a lion will retreat from a human who comes too close and enters his danger zone. But, when he can retreat no longer and the human still advances, the lion will turn and approach the human. A lion trainer takes advantage of this and moves toward the lion in his cage. The animal retreats, as is its nature, to the back of the cage as the lion trainer advances. When the lion can go no farther, he turns and, in accordance with his nature, snarls and advances on the trainer in a straight line. Because the trainer is aware of this, a lion's platform is placed between him and the lion. The lion, approaching in a straight line, climbs the platform to get at the human trainer. At this point the trainer moves out of the lion's danger zone and the lion stops advancing. Audiences imagine that the trainer's gun, whip, and chair are holding a dangerous beast at bay.

For centuries, actors were aware that the distance of the stage from the audience can create illusions. At a distance, it is easy to lie with exaggerated motions of the body. Frequently, the public sphere is used to impress the audience, not necessarily to tell the truth. (I suggest you watch the 1934 propaganda film *Triumph of the Will* and notice how Hitler staged his speeches to the German people.) Stage actors need to use stylized, affected, and symbolic movements (that is, gross movements using the entire body) to communicate emotions. The gestures of traditional stage have been refined, studied, and practiced for years. Actually we could say that there is a cultural attachment involved with gestures of the stage. An illustration is the Japanese kabuki theater, which contains symbolic culture-oriented gestures (half of which we Westerners do not understand). Television and motion pictures combine long shots and close-ups. Up close, a movement of the lips and the blink of an eye will convey a message as much as the gross movement of the body does in a long shot. Close-ups of gross movements are misinterpreted. This is probably why there is difficulty adapting movies and television to the stage and vice versa.

In conclusion, this chapter and the applied exercises are intended merely to introduce the reader to the fascinating work being done in body language, kinesics, small group ecology, and proxemics. Competencies in these areas are important for many careers that require nonverbal communication. Even the criminal justice field uses body-language specialists for jury selection (and reading jurors during trial), witnesses, and understanding the judge's gestures.

12.1 APPLIED EXERCISE: NONVERBAL COMMUNICATION OF OTHERS

1. Observation: at a singles' club/bar, observe the nonverbal communication between people.
2. Develop a list of ways that people telegraph their interest/disinterest in one another.
3. Focus on:

    * gestures
    * eye contact
    * facial expressions
    * vocal behavior
    * trunk and shoulders
    * arm and wrist
    * hand and fingers
    * hip
    * leg and ankle
    * foot and neck
    * overall posture
    * general presentation of self (including clothing)
    * touch
    * personal space

4. Summarize your observation and see if you can come up with unstated but important rules about nonverbal communication (include gender differentiation).
5. Note how the same gestures, etc., would be interpreted at home, in the street, or at school/church.
6. Discuss the gender similarities and differences.

12.2 APPLIED EXERCISE: NONVERBAL COMMUNICATION—SELF-ASSESSMENT

1. Interview a close friend or relative and find out how he or she knows from your nonverbal communication when you are:

    - angry
    - sad
    - disgusted
    - fearful
    - depressed
    - happy
    - surprised

    These are part of our genetic makeup; these are some of our basic physical reactions.

2. Ask them to focus on:

    - gestures
    - eye contact
    - facial expressions
    - vocal behavior
    - trunk and shoulders
    - arm and wrist
    - hand and fingers
    - hip
    - leg and ankle
    - foot and neck
    - overall posture
    - general presentation of self (including clothing)
    - touch
    - personal space

3. Summarize their observations and note how many things are unconscious.

12.3 APPLIED EXERCISE: NONVERBAL COMMUNICATION—SPACE

1. Observe your dog or cat for at least 30 minutes.
2. Describe your pet and how you communicate with it.
3. Identify and list the gestures that you read from your pet.
4. Identify and describe any territory elements.
5. Identify and list the gestures that you transmit to your pet and note the behavior.

12.4 APPLIED EXERCISE: NONVERBAL COMMUNICATION—SILENT MEAL

1. Have a meal set up buffet style and invite the group to eat.
2. As people enter, instruct them to put away cell phones, iPads, laptops, all technology.
3. Instruct everyone that there is to be no verbal or written communication.
4. Allow the group to enjoy the meal without talking for at least 25 minutes.

Debrief

- Summarize their observations.
- Describe how the group passed the time.
- Develop a list of ways that people telegraph their messages.
- Share feelings that people experienced as time passed.

NOTE

1. Hall, E.T. (1966). *The Hidden Dimension*. New York: Doubleday. Also, (1959). *The Silent Language*. New York: Doubleday.

CHAPTER 13

NONVIOLENT COMMUNICATION

By Michiko Kuroda, Mercy College
International Relations and Diplomacy Program

WHAT IS THE CONNECTION BETWEEN OUR WORDS AND OUR EMOTIONS? HOW DOES LANGUAGE CONNECT WITH OUR FEELINGS, NEEDS, AND CONCERNS?

INTRODUCTION TO NONVIOLENT COMMUNICATION

NONVIOLENT COMMUNICATION AND LIFE ENERGY

Everything we did in our life, everything we do in our life, and everything we will do in our life is for one reason. What could it be?

Discussion 1: What do you think it could be?

The answer to the question above, according to Mr. Thom Bond, Certified Non-Violent Communication (NVC) Trainer, is "to meet our needs." This is in accordance with Dr. Marshall B. Rosenberg,[1] who "identified a specific approach to communicating—both speaking and listening—that leads us to give from the heart, connecting us with ourselves and with each other in a way that allows our natural compassion to flourish."[2]

Discussion 2: Can you think about someone who has no needs?

The answer is "No one who is alive." If someone does not have a need for anything, it could be argued that he or she is not alive. As long as human beings are alive, they have needs and their needs constitute life energy. Needs or values are the life energy that NVC pays attention to. Rosenberg used the term "nonviolent" as Mahatma Gandhi did, referring to our natural state of compassion where violence has subsided from the heart.[3] NVC focuses on words and suggests that using violent words often leads to hurt and pain, either for others or ourselves.[4] NVC can also be called compassionate communication.

In NVC, we focus on four major aspects: observe, feel, need, and request. This chapter focuses on two of the major aspects: feelings and needs. NVC practice and training helps us observe and listen to others and ourselves, thereby enabling us to understand situations in a deeper way. NVC practice and approach facilitates conflict resolution and management. In my personal experience of practicing NVC over the years, I came to understand others and, most importantly, myself with regard to what I want and what my heart desires. In my international career, NVC helped me to identify solutions for conflicts among people from different backgrounds. Figure 13.1 illustrates the concept of NVC.

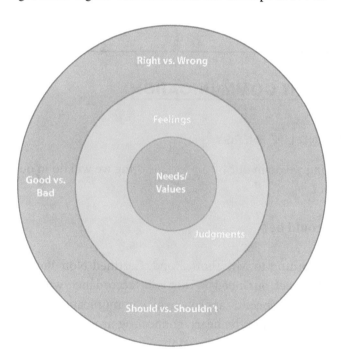

Fig. 13.1 The Concept of NVC and Our Life

Adapted from: Thom Bond / New York Center for NVC.

Judgments

We are surrounded by judgments, which include right versus wrong, good versus bad, and should versus shouldn't. There is nothing inherently wrong with these judgments and thoughts; they are simply ways to explain how we grow, learn, and live our lives. They help us to understand our behaviors. For many they represent the first ways we learn. For example, "Do not touch it! Do not eat that! Do not go there!" These are judgments communicated by parents and others for the safety of the child.

Feelings

The second circle shows feelings. People have feelings to show the extent to which they meet the needs. If their needs are met, they show fulfilled feelings. If their needs are not met, unfulfilled feelings will show up. Feelings are therefore giving us a message in connection to our needs. Naturally, there are many levels of feelings between fulfilled and unfulfilled; these will depend on the extent to which needs are met. It may be helpful to go through the list of feelings in order to experience the wide range that human beings have.

The center of the circle shows needs or values. This represents the needs or values of a universal nature. For example, when you say you want or need a car, the car itself is not a need or a value. The car is a strategy to meet your need/value, which may be movement, comfort, or status. It is important to understand and distinguish the differences between the needs/values and strategies. Needs or values do not contradict each other; strategies do. Therefore, if you are able to identify the true needs/values, you will be better able to design an effective strategy to help resolve conflicts.

- Fulfilled Feelings: Look at the Feeling Sheet at the end of the chapter. Observe the list of Fulfilled Feelings. Go through one feeling to another. Observe that we could have many different feelings. Identify all the feelings that you may have in your life. You may wish to use this list to articulate your feelings.
- Unfulfilled Feelings: Now look at the list of Unfulfilled Feelings. Review the list and observe that we could have so many kinds of unfulfilled feelings. Notice that each feeling is different and has different implications. It is important and helpful to feel your feelings as you practice NVC in your life.

Check the list and look at the words such as "abandoned," "intimidated," "harassed," and "ignored."[5] While we use them in our daily life to express our feelings, these do not necessarily represent feelings. Rather, these words indicate actions. Action words are action-oriented rather than feeling words. When using these words, the focus is on the person who took action; in fact, you may be blaming the person, rather than focusing on your own feelings. It is very important to focus on feelings so that we can identify needs and values. When you say, "I feel abandoned," what are your real feelings? In this case, you may feel sad, lonely, angry, or disappointed. In this case, *abandoned* is an action done by someone else; *sad*, etc., is a feeling of the abandoned person.

It is important to understand and to take responsibility for our feelings. The more we do, the more we understand ourselves. Feelings give us information regarding which of our needs are being met. Therefore, we will understand our needs by doing this. My experience was that NVC practices have given me clarification and a deeper understanding about myself. This enabled me to focus on what I really wanted to pursue.

Discussion 3: How many of you believe that men have no feelings? Raise your hand. How many of you believe that women have too many feelings? Raise your hands.

The truth is that both men and women have feelings. It is likely that men are not used to expressing or exploring their feelings and women may be more used to expressing them. Simply put, men and women have different relationships with feelings. Given that everyone has feelings, it might be worth exploring them so that both men and women could learn about their needs and those of others.

NEEDS[6]

PERSONAL STORY 1: SAFETY

When I started my practice of NVC, my daughter was 18 or 19 years old and boarding at college. When she was home on vacation, she often went out to see her friends. I had no idea where she went and with whom she was spending time. She usually came home very late, sometimes as late as 3:00 AM. While I had trust in her, I was very worried that she could get in trouble, especially in NYC, which could be dangerous for young people. I constantly called her or sent text messages. Very often, she did not respond. I was worried, so I kept calling. One day, when she came home at midnight, we had a conversation like this.

- Daughter (D): "Mommy, what are you doing? You know that I go out with my friends. Why do you keep calling me?"
- Me: "I know you are with your friends but I do not know where you are. I was really, really worried. As parent, I need to know where you are and when you come home."
- D: "Why? When I am off college, you have no idea where I am. I am not a baby any more. Why do you try to control me? Don't you trust me?"
- Me: "I have no intention to control you, and I do not. I trust you of course! You are my daughter. But I am really worried about you. We live in New York City where a number of dangerous incidents happen. We never know what happens. I am concerned about your safety. You are my daughter; I love you. I would like you to grow and have a great future. I care about your future. Just let me know that you are OK and when you come home."
- D: "I see. OK. Thank you for your love. Thank you for caring about my safety and future."

After this conversation, I decided not to send text messages to her. I told myself she should be OK. Most interestingly, since then, she was the one to send me messages saying where she was and when she was coming home. I was very much amazed that it was the power of NVC that made this difference.

PERSONAL STORY 2: PURPOSE

I was very proud to work for the United Nations, as I considered it my calling. I had a sense of purpose, which was very important. Over the course of my 30-year career, I developed my mission statement. This helped me to focus on my mission. During my UN career I traveled all over the world. I always put other people's interests first. I even risked my life. I was fully satisfied with my career. Therefore, when my retirement day was approaching, I was very sad. I thought I would become nobody, as my need for service or purpose was very important to me; I believe I was born to work or to serve. On my last day at the UN, as I visited the Mediation Room established by the former Secretary-General Dag Hammarskjöld, I received a message saying, "Stay connected." I felt better. A few months later I was asked to work again at the UN on a short-term contract basis. I felt happy and relieved. Several months later, I started to teach at Mercy College. When I shared my working experiences at the United Nations, I saw my students' eyes shine. At that moment I realized I was still living my mission. I realized I do not have to be working in the UN to meet my need for purpose, as I was helping my students on their way to become peace builders. I was able to renew my commitment toward my purpose in peace building.

EXERCISE I: THE T-BONE

1. Think about a time when someone said something to you that you were not happy with.
2. Remember the sentence? Write down on a sheet of paper the sentence that made you unhappy. Quote it.
3. Draw a T-bone. On the left side, write down "F."

"You are so stupid!"

F	N

4. Try to remember how you felt at that moment. Look at the Feelings Sheet and identify how you felt at that moment. (You may find more than one.) Be calm. Reflect on it.
5. Now, on the right side of the T-bone, write down "N."
6. Look at the Needs Sheet and identify what your needs were at that moment. (You may find more than one.) Be calm. Reflect on it.
7. What do you think about it?
8. Now, draw a T-bone again. Write down the same quote. Write down "F" on the left side and "N" on the right side again.
9. Look at the Feelings Sheet. This time, try to guess the feelings of the person who said that sentence to you. Just make a guess. It does not have to be correct. Go through the sheet and write them down.
10. Then, look at the Needs Sheet. Now guess which needs the person was trying to meet. Just make a guess. It does not have to be correct. Go through the sheet and write them down.
11. How do you feel?

Make sure to have a post-exercise discussion. It will be an effective way to help students learn and understand the importance of identifying feelings and needs. Ask whether there has been any shift vis-à-vis the person the students are reflecting on. If some students experienced shifts in how they feel about the past exchange, encourage them to share their experiences. Most likely they have new perspectives about the person they previously considered in a totally negative way. You will notice the powerful effect of sharing on students' learning.

In the second part of Exercise I, you gave empathy to the person who made the statement that you were not happy with. In the first part of Exercise I, you gave self-empathy, which means you gave empathy to yourself. You were identifying your feelings and needs. This exercise is a must for NVC beginners. While it is quite simple, you will understand and experience the impact of empathy.

HOMEWORK 1: T-bone Exercise (feelings and needs)
Do the T-bone Exercise three times a day until the next class meeting.

It is highly recommended that students share their experiences of this homework in the class. They may also discuss lessons learned from this homework.

Judgments

Judgments also give us an indication about our needs, whether met or not met. When our judgments show up, our focus is on thinking about good versus bad, right versus wrong, or should versus shouldn't. While judgments do not necessarily connect with our life energy, translating judgments into feelings and then into needs may help us clarify our layers of needs.

HOMEWORK 2: Judgments Journal
Write down three judgment statements each day.
Identify and write down your feelings and what needs were not met.

By doing this homework for one week, students should become sharply aware of how judgments could be translated into feelings and needs. Has anyone noticed there are layers of needs? Some needs could be the strategies to meet higher needs or values. Logging judgments will be helpful to identify different types of needs.

HOMEWORK 3: Needs Assessment about Your Needs

1. Take the Needs Sheet.
2. For each need, on a scale of 1 to 10, write to the left of each word the level of how much your need has been met.
3. On a scale of 1 to 10, write to the right of each word the level of how important your need is.
4. Do this for all the needs words.
5. Think about all the words and how you've ranked them.
6. Identify three needs that have been mostly met.
7. Identify three needs that have been least met.
8. Identify three needs that are most important to you.
9. Identify three needs that are least important to you.
10. Consider them. What do you think about these lists?
11. Discuss your comments and reflection in the class.

Discuss the findings in the class. The students may have discovered something about themselves that they had not thought about before. While the list of needs mostly met or least met could change, they tend to indicate the areas they need to work on to better enjoy life. I put this data into an Excel sheet from which I made a graph, which clearly showed the trends in my needs met and unmet, and importance of those met. I became aware of which needs I need to focus on in order to make my life fulfilling.

Empathy

Let's discuss the meaning of empathy and how we can practice empathy. Empathy means:

- be present, or empty (or open) in your mind
- focus on the other person(s) (not on yourself)
- make no judgment and be ready to receive a message

Therefore, when you give empathy you have to be present for the person, focus on the person, and listen without judgment.

Empathy is very powerful. When people receive empathy they feel they were heard and understood, which creates space. This may lead to their understanding, deep connection, and even healing. Therefore, the person you are with may not need solutions, conflict resolution, or problem solving. It may be enough to receive empathy.

Empathy is different from sympathy. Empathy implies that you receive what the other person speaks to you and experience the feelings of the person. Sympathy means that you are judging what the person says and how you feel about it. For example, with sympathy, your response may be, "I am sorry," "You poor thing," or "That's terrible!"

Empathy focuses on the other person; sympathy focuses on you. In our daily life, even if you have a good intention to help your friends, you may be trying to give reassurance or fix-it advice.[7]

Exercise II: Non-Empathetic Practice
Quote: "I look like a pig."
Non-Empathy Examples

- Comparing: "If you look like a pig, I look like an elephant."
- Advising: "How about doing the vegetable diet. You may be able to lose weight easily."
- Educating: "I have an idea of what it means to look like a pig. What will be the impact on our health? Let's look at the website www.healthylook.com."
- Consoling: "I love the way you look. You look like a person full of care and love."
- Shutting down: "What are you talking about? So what?"
- Sympathizing: "Sorry to hear that."
- Information gathering: "I am wondering how many people belong to a category that looks like a pig. Let us conduct a survey at Mercy College."
- Explaining: "It is possible that your mother gave you too much food when you were a child."

You may have noticed that this is what we usually do while trying to listen to others. Instead, we should spend the time to consider how best to respond. Now we will have a practice of giving empathy, but in silence.

Exercise III: Silent Empathy

1. Divide students into pairs (A and B).
2. A will share a story; B will listen actively with empathy. B should give empathy silently; therefore, B should not nod or use body gesture to show whether B agrees or not.
3. A will speak for 5 minutes; B will just listen.
4. When the time is over, switch the roles.
5. The class will have a group discussion on how it went and lessons learned, and make any observations.

Make sure to have post-exercise discussion in the class. You will notice that it is very hard to stay silent while the partner is speaking because we are used to interrupting without listening carefully. We may also tend to be judgmental and keep thinking about how to respond. That is not empathy. To give empathy, you have to be present by emptying your mind of judgments. If you practice giving empathy, you will start understanding how people feel and think. Let us now start practicing giving empathy or receiving and listening with empathy.

Exercise IV: Empathy Circle

1. Make a group of four or five students.
2. One person will share a story.
3. Everybody else will listen and give empathy, which means they will empty their mind and listen without any judgments.
4. From time to time those who are listening will acknowledge feelings and needs, from the list, in a question form. In other words, you will take a guess at the person's feelings and needs.
5. Go slowly. Do not rush. Acknowledge one feeling or need at a time.
6. Give no advice, no solution, or agreement. Just listen.
7. Continue until the person who is speaking feels complete.
8. Take turns.
9. After everybody finishes, give feedback to each other.

It is highly recommended that the class conduct Empathy Circles from time to time. You will be amazed how students will gain the ability to listen to each other with empathy and without being judgmental.

NVC and Conflict Resolution

Empathy is the core of NVC practice: the ability to understand and articulate your feelings and needs and to understand and articulate the other person's feelings and needs. Ideally both parties should demonstrate this ability. This is the premise that facilitates conflict resolution. Once it is done you may not even need to discuss a solution—one may come naturally. Table 13.1 illustrates this basis.

Table 13.1: Basis for Conflict Resolution in NVC

I	You
I understand and articulate *my* feelings and needs. I understand and articulate *your* feelings and needs.	You understand and articulate *your* feelings and needs. You understand and articulate *my* feelings and needs.

When engaging in conflict resolution and mediation, spend time to create space in order to ensure you understand and articulate the parties' feelings and needs. Then you may be able to facilitate conflict resolution or even conflict transformation.

Anger

Discussion 4: What do you think about the following statement?
"People do not make us angry, how we think makes us angry." (Marshall Rosenberg)

Stimulate versus Cause

In NVC we take responsibility for our feelings and needs. It means that our feelings are not caused by others' words or behaviors. In other words, we are not the victims of others, as we will have a role. We may be stimulated by how people speak or act. We therefore have a choice of how to think, act, or react. Rosenberg gives suggestions as to how to handle anger by understanding the meaning of anger, rather than managing anger. Because anger is a very strong feeling, it is helpful in determining what a person needs. This is a very different approach from managing anger, which attempts to reduce or suppress anger by calming down. In NVC practice we welcome anger because it gives indications as to which needs we are trying to meet.

Judgments behind Anger

Anger is a feeling behind which there are usually strong judgments, such as "should" or "shouldn't." You may be automatically thinking, "He should not do this; she should do that." In such a situation, explore your feelings. You may be sad, disappointed, or scared. Then feel your feelings and identify your unmet needs. You will experience how the feeling of anger is guiding you to what you really want. Now let's do an exercise for Anger Process, which is beyond Anger Management. You will understand the difference by doing this exercise.

EXERCISE V: ANGER PROCESS

Everyone pairs up. Find a situation that makes you angry.

- Step 1: Notice. Are you tense? Are you thinking that someone should or should not be doing something? Are you feeling agitated and uneasy? What is your need?
- Step 2: Stop, shhh, quiet. Still angry? Don't speak.
- Step 3: Make space. Excuse yourself, run!
- Step 4: Identify my moralistic or should/shouldn't thinking.
- Step 5: Identify underlying feelings such as agitation, fear, frustration.
- Step 6: Identify and connect to your unmet needs.
- Step 7: Think of requests you can make of yourself or others.
- Step 8: Debrief.

Make sure that each student shares his or her stories and lessons learned. Enjoy the power of sharing, which will facilitate deep learning.

PERSONAL STORY 4: ANGER PROCESS

For summer vacation I went home to Japan to see my mother. In an attempt to be helpful I spent a lot of time in the kitchen cooking meals for the family. One day my mother asked me, "How do you feel about being a housewife?" I said "What?" I was very annoyed and angry. I felt angry emotions coming up my body. I said, "I am not a housewife!" I left the kitchen, as I was very, very angry. I was MAD! All my judgments bubbled to the surface. I thought about my childhood when my mother told me she went to the first Women's College in the country and became a science teacher. "When I married your father," she told me, "he said I should quit the job, and I did. Now I regret it! It is very important for you to have a job and have your own income." I never forgot this conversation with her. Later in life I decided to have my own job to secure my independence. I wanted to tell her that it was because of her that I became a career woman. I was never a housewife. Why did she ask that? She should not say this! I was so angry, I burst into tears. Then I remembered the anger process. I went through it step by step. I was able to process my anger and connect to my unmet needs, which were needs for respect, recognition, and choice. For her, she had needs for care and support, and to understand and be understood. Once I clarified all of these needs I went back to the kitchen to talk with my mother. We had a compassionate conversation. I was so grateful to my mother for protecting me. I realized that behind my independence I received her strong support.

Hearing "No"

Now that you learned about various aspects of NVC it is possible you are ready to hear *no* from others—partners, colleagues, friends, families, teachers, and yourself. We understand that when someone answers with a no, it means he or she is looking for yes to something else in an attempt to meet his or her needs. When we hear no, we can get stuck on our strategy or we can find it an opportunity to continue dialogue by showing empathic inquiry. This gives us an opportunity to practice being in touch with our value of mutuality and consideration of the needs of everyone involved. When we hear no from the other person, we have an opportunity to understand the needs of the person.

Exercise VI: Hearing No

Make your partner respond with a *no* response to the following sentences. Then, do not react. Give empathy to the person in an attempt to find your partner's needs.

1. Would you like to go out for pizza tonight?
2. Could you help me clean up these dishes?
3. How about going to Paris next summer?
4. (Make your own sentence.)

Discuss this exercise in the class. If you are able to listen to and hear no, you are getting used to using NVC in your life. Enjoy the exercise.

NVC Appreciation

In our habitual way of appreciation, we may say "You are great!" or "You did a great job!" which is about judgments. In NVC appreciation, you will state the following:

- Make an observation of what the person did
- Tell how you felt when the person did it (as above)
- Tell what kinds of needs are met

You may notice that NVC appreciation, if practiced well, will help you better connect to people with whom you have a relationship. Enjoy this practice.

Conclusions

This chapter focused on feelings and needs. The course Managing Human Conflict II will discuss observing and requesting in detail, which will include negotiation and conflict resolution for connecting. Through this you will be able to experience conflict transformation. All of these aspects will enable you to practice NVC in your daily life. Feelings and needs constitute the core of NVC practices, which may have already changed your life and conflict perspectives.

REFERENCES

Marshall B. Rosenberg. (2003). *Nonviolent Communication: A Language of Life*. Encinitas, CA: Puddle Dancer Press.

Marshall Rosenberg. (2005). *Amazing Power of Anger: Beyond Anger Management—Finding the Gift (Nonviolent Communication Guides)*. Encinitas, CA: Puddle Dancer Press.

John Gray. (1992). *Men Are from Mars, Women Are from Venus: The Classic Guide to Understanding the Opposite Sex.* New York: Harper Collins Publishers.

Michiko Kuroda and Kumar Rupersinghe (Co-editors). (1992). *Early Warning and Conflict Resolution*. London and New York: McMillan and St. Martin's Press.

NOTES

1. Marshall B. Rosenberg, *Nonviolent Communication: A Language of Life*, Puddle Dancer Press, Encinitas, CA, 2003.
2. Rosenberg, Ibid.
3. Rosenberg, Ibid., 2.
4. Rosenberg, Ibid., 3.
5. Other non-feeling words are abused, attacked, belittled, betrayed, blamed, bullied, coerced, cornered, criticized, discounted, diminished, disliked, distrusted, dumped on, harassed, hassled, ignored, insulted, and intimidated.
6. "To embody" or "Embodiment" means that you stay with the particular feeling for a while. Feel the feeling. Meditate on it. Think of a time in the past when you did this.
7. Rosenberg, p. 92.

APPENDIX

LIST I: FEELINGS LIST

Fulfilled Feelings (feelings when our needs are met)

AFFECTIONATE

compassionate

friendly

fond

loving

open-hearted

sympathetic

tender

warm

CONFIDENT

empowered

open

proud

safe

secure

INSPIRED

amazed

awed

wonder

ENGAGED

absorbed

alert

curious

engrossed

enchanted

entranced

fascinated

interested

intrigued

involved

spellbound

stimulated

REFRESHED

enlivened

rejuvenated

renewed

rested

restored

revived

GRATEFUL

appreciative

moved

thankful

touched

EXCITED

amazed

animated

ardent

aroused

dazzled

eager

energetic

enthusiastic

giddy

invigorated

lively

passionate

surprised

vibrant

JOYFUL

amused

delighted

glad

happy

jubilant

pleased

tickled

overjoyed

EXHILARATED

blissful

ecstatic

elated

enthralled

exuberant

radiant

rapturous

thrilled

electrified

euphoric

overjoyed

PEACEFUL

calm

clearheaded

comfortable

centered

content

equanimity

fulfilled

mellow

quiet

relaxed

relieved

satisfied

serene

still

tranquil

trusting

HOPEFUL

expectant

encouraged

optimistic

inspired

http://nycnvc.org/needs.htm

Unfulfilled Feelings (feelings when our needs are not met)

AFRAID

apprehensive
dread
fearful
foreboding
frightened
mistrustful
panicked
petrified
scared
suspicious
terrified
wary
worried

ANNOYED

aggravated
dismayed
disgruntled
displeased
exasperated
frustrated
impatient
irritated
irked

ANGER

angry
enraged
furious
incensed
indignant
irate
livid
outraged
resentful

CONFUSED

ambivalent
baffled
bewildered
dazed
hesitant
lost
mystified
perplexed
puzzled
torn

DISQUIET

agitated
alarmed
discombobulated
disconcerted
disturbed
perturbed
rattled
restless
shocked
startled
surprised
troubled
turbulent
turmoil
uncomfortable
uneasy
unnerved
unsettled
upset

EMBARRASSED

ashamed
chagrined

flustered
guilty
mortified
self-conscious

FATIGUE

beat
burnt out
depleted
exhausted
lethargic
listless
sleepy
tired
weary
worn out

AVERSION

animosity
appalled
contempt
disgusted
dislike
hate
horrified
hostile
repulsed

TENSE

anxious
cranky
distressed
distraught
edgy
fidgety

frazzled
irritable
jittery
nervous
overwhelmed
restless
stressed out

VULNERABLE

fragile
guarded
helpless
insecure
leery
reserved
sensitive
shaky

PAIN

agony
anguished
bereaved
devastated
grief
heartbroken
hurt
lonely
miserable
regretful
remorseful

SAD

depressed
dejected
despair
despondent

disappointed
discouraged
disheartened
forlorn
gloomy
heavy hearted
hopeless
melancholy
unhappy
wretched

DISCONNECTED

alienated
aloof
apathetic
bored
cold
detached
distant
distracted
indifferent
numb
removed
withdrawn

YEARNING

envious
jealous
longing
nostalgic
pining
wistful

http://nycnvc.org/needs.htm

LIST II: NEEDS LIST

CONNECTION
Acceptance
Affection
Appreciation
Belonging
Cooperation
Communication
Closeness
Community
Companionship
Compassion
Consideration
Consistency
Empathy
Inclusion
Intimacy
Love
Mutuality
Nurturing
Respect/Self-respect
Safety
Security
Shared Reality
Stability
Support
To know and be known
To see and be seen
To understand and be understood
Trust
Warmth

HONESTY
Authenticity
Integrity
Presence

PLAY
Joy
Humor
Fun
Adventure

PEACE
Beauty
Communion
Ease
Equality
Harmony
Inspiration
Order

PHYSICAL WELL-BEING
Air
Food
Movement/exercise
Rest/sleep
Sexual expression
Safety
Shelter
Touch
Water

MEANING
Awareness
Celebration of life
Challenge
Clarity
Competence
Consciousness
Contribution
Creativity
Discovery
Efficacy
Effectiveness
Growth
Hope
Learning
Mourning
Participation
Purpose
Self-expression
Stimulation
To matter
Understanding

AUTONOMY
Choice
Freedom
Independence
Space
Spontaneity

ww.nycnvc.org

CHAPTER 14

FAMILY AND BIRTH ORDER

By Lindsay Astor and Dorothy Balancio

HOW DOES YOUR POSITION IN YOUR FAMILY AFFECT YOUR COMMUNICATION STYLE?

FAMILY: BIRTH ORDER

Family life is a universal experience. Yet no two people share the exact same experience, partly because of the unique place we have in the family system. Our experiences in our family of origin serve as a powerful perceptual filter as we relate to the world. Family of origin refers to the family or families in which a person is raised and is generally thought to be the earliest and most powerful influence on our personality. Actually, we could say that the family of origin provides a blueprint for our personalities and communication style. The focus of this chapter is on siblings and birth order. People have a need to belong. Therefore, when we are born into the family is significant. The family is the first group we enter. Family is our first social unit. We could say that family is a unique way to manage people and to manage conflict because it offers a different way to understand others and ourselves.

Take a moment and reflect on your relationship with your siblings. These relationships reflect individual personalities, talents, and traits. For example, being the oldest sibling might mean you became the family chauffeur, were the first to get a job, and were the one from whom others could borrow money. Because of birth order siblings act as teachers, playmates, confidants, peers, and friends. For most people, the sibling relationship is the longest-lasting relationship in their lives and cannot be terminated (even if the adult interaction is limited, most keep abreast of each other through a third party). The sibling relationship is involuntary. It is estimated that 80% of all individuals spend at least one-third of their lives with their siblings.[1]

Remember that all we are offering here are tendencies that apply to people born into certain positions in their families. These characteristics won't apply to everyone, and there are exceptions. Personality, gender, life experiences, family size, spacing of siblings, education, social class, ethnicity, regionalism, and genes influence who we are. However, these descriptions can prove useful as you look to gain better insight into yourself as well as the people around you. (In fact, there are management and marketing seminars that use birth order characteristics in their businesses.)

Birth order will add another component to understanding our interactions. It will add another dimension to our introspective journey to negotiation and managing people in our relationships. Look at characteristics that researchers attribute to:

- firstborn (the achiever)
- middles (the diplomat/negotiator)
- lastborn (the baby, a charmer, people person, great delegator)
- the only (the movers and shakers)

Keep in mind the distinctions tend to blur as we age. However, personalities are influenced by birth order (and in some cases, it pertains to the extended family). A general understanding can add to our skill set in communicating with others. Do not stereotype them, and do not focus on the negative expectations—focus on the positive! Maximize the other's strengths and minimize the problems.

In 1923 Alfred Adler, a psychiatrist, wrote that a person's "position in the family leaves an indelible stamp" on his or her life. Subsequent research has shown that while birth order does indeed affect a child, it does not automatically shape personality. If it did, life would be more predictable and less interesting.

14.1 APPLIED EXERCISE: BIRTH ORDER

1. Divide the class into groups by their place in the family: the firstborn, the middle, the youngest, or the only.
2. Have each group discuss the advantages and disadvantages of being in that position in their family.
3. Have each group describe the other three groups.
4. Have each group come up with a list of words/phrases that describe what it was like to be in that position in the family.

Debrief

Use the four descriptions to encourage the discussion.

Give the following overview of the firstborn child, middle child, youngest child, and only child after each group reports on the advantages and disadvantages of their birth order.

If you were to try to sell something to a customer, you would approach:

- **the firstborn child** and **only child** in an organized way (the onlys take time, but get things done like the firstborns)
- **the middle child** by giving them options/letting them choose and make up their own minds
- **the youngest child** by getting to know them well (they rely on their instincts/intuition and go with people they feel are the best fit)

After sharing the groups' descriptions, read the generalizations that follow.

THE FIRSTBORN CHILD

Conscientious and achievement oriented; as the first out of the cradle, they tend to be up to the task with all challenges.

- Enter the adult world and are excited by adult approval; strive to please others
- Aware of authority
- Attuned to the adult world for assurance and acceptance
- Organized in their mental process/in their mind (serious list makers)
- Prefer order and routine (good thought processers; keep things in order)
- Like established format/routine/doing things the correct/established way
- Cautious about new ideas (winners challenge or compete/losers do not challenge)
- Driven in accomplishing goals that they set for themselves (initially they may be quieter, but later on they become more talkative about accomplishing their goals)
- Driven toward success and stardom in their given field (21 of the first 23 U.S. astronauts were firstborns/onlys)
- Focused on their personal achievement and growth; inner commitment
- Deep sense of self-worth/leader/boss (bossy); enjoy being in control
- Perfectionist/afraid of failure/do not take criticism well/high expectation for themselves and others around them (will avoid any chance for criticism)

Innate Strengths

The firstborn is often used to being the center of attention; he has Mom and Dad to himself before siblings arrive (oldest children enjoy about 3,000 hours more quality time with their parents between ages 4 and 13 than the next sibling will get, found a study from Brigham Young University in Provo, Utah). "Many parents spend more time reading and explaining things to the firstborns. It's not as easy when other kids come into the picture," says Frank Farley, Ph.D., a psychologist at Temple University in Philadelphia, who has studied personality and human development for decades. "That undivided attention may have a lot to do with why firstborns tend to be overachievers," he explains. They look for ways to gain back the undivided attention/approval they got used to receiving before their siblings came along. In addition to usually scoring higher on IQ tests and generally getting more education than their brothers and sisters, firstborns tend to outlearn their siblings (firstborns were more likely to make at least $100,000 annually compared to their siblings, according to a recent Careerbuilder.com survey).

Common Challenges

Success comes at a price: firstborns tend to be type-A personalities who never cut themselves any slack. "They often have an intense fear of failure, so nothing they accomplish feels good enough," says Michelle P. Maidenberg, Ph.D., a child and family therapist in White Plains, New York. And because they dread making a misstep, oldest kids tend to stick to the straight and narrow. "They're typically inflexible—they don't like change and are hesitant to step out of their comfort zone," she explains.

Because firstborns are often given a lot of responsibility at home—whether it's helping with chores or watching over younger siblings—they can be quick to take charge (and can be bossy when they do). That burden can lead to excess stress for a child who already feels pressure to be perfect. These firstborns sometimes are like little grown-ups: it is easy to give them responsibility, easy to trust them.

Necessary Nurturing

Firstborns are constantly receiving encouragement for their achievements, but they also need to know it is okay if they don't succeed at everything, says psychologist Kevin Lerman, Ph.D., *The Birth Order Book*.

THE MIDDLE CHILD: THE DIPLOMAT/NEGOTIATOR

- Independent minded
- Most independent problem-solving
- Risk taker—can afford to gamble (e.g., ride a bike without training wheels)
- Try harder
- Devil's advocate
- Guilt tripper
- Investigator/investigate people (i.e., part groups like a hot knife going through butter)
- Answer a question with a question
- Aware of others' feelings (i.e., know how to get people going)
- Sensitivity for others—but, they are the mystery child
- Friends become very important; create their identity through outside groups
- Intuitive in social situations/blessed; better training for real life
- Most likely to become whatever the older siblings are not
- (middles bounce off the kids directly above them, deliberately taking on traits and interests that will save them from having to compete)

The middle children are born too late to get privileges and special treatment that firstborns seem to inherit. When another child arrives, middle children lose the bonanza that the youngest enjoy—usually a variety of privileges due to a relaxing of the disciplinary reins.

Researchers who study birth order say that middle children are the hardest to describe because they are influenced by so many variables, especially the:

- personality of the older
- personality of younger siblings
- number of years between them

Innate Strengths

Middleborns are go-with-the-flow types; once a younger sibling arrives, they must learn to constantly negotiate and compromise in order to fit in with everyone. A study by Dr. Sulloway notes that middle children score higher in agreeableness than both their older and younger siblings. Because they receive less attention at home, middle children tend to forge stronger bonds with friends and be less tied to the family than their brothers and sisters. For example, they would be eager to take a trip with a family member or want to sleep at a friend's house, according to Linda Dunlap, Ph.D., professor of psychology at Marist College, Poughkeepsie, New York.

Common Challenges

Middle children were the babies of the family, until they were dethroned by a new sibling. They often are aware that they do not get as much parental attention as their trailblazing older sibling or the beloved youngest. The middle child tends to feel like their needs and wants are ignored. "Middle kids are in a different position in a family because they think that they are not valued" and "It's easy for them to be left out and get lost in the shuffle," says Dr. Maidenberg. There is some validity to their complaint. A survey by BabyWebsite.com, a British parenting resource, found that a third of parents with three children admit to giving their middle child far less attention than they give their other two.

Necessary Nurturing

Middle children complain that they are not heard within the family. Suggestions: let this child make decisions (such as choosing the restaurant or movie that everyone goes to). It is important to help middle children develop self-esteem by recognizing their talents and their individuality. It is important for all children to feel special in their parents' eyes and to have a quality they feel is valued in the family. In the case of the middle child, it is especially hard to carve out that place in the family. Middle children may feel they have no particular role in the family to define themselves. Therefore, friends become very important to middle children. Outside the family, they find it easier to forge their own identities. They develop friendship skills that firstborns lack, and they learn to be good team players and club members. This will empower the middle child who is frequently deferring to the oldest one's wants and the youngest one's needs. The middle child can often feel squeezed out by their siblings: The older sibling gets more responsibility and opportunities, while the younger sibling is coddled and babied.

The middle children get lots of **practice at negotiating conflicts**, since they have to deal with it in both directions. Lacking the benefit of the exceptions parents make for their firstborns and their youngest, middle children may learn to negotiate, compromise, and collaborate—valuable life skills that will help them succeed (they get better training for real life than firstborns and babies do).

Their flexibility and sociability means they will often end up being the kind of laid-back people others like to be around. They also usually show strength when it comes to compromise and coalition building.

As a result: a middle child often makes a very good romantic partner. Since middle children are least likely to have been spoiled in any way, they are most likely willing to work hard to create a happy and meaningful relationship.

Pitfall: middle children typically hate conflict. They have experienced enough conflict and therefore do all they can to avoid it. That is a dangerous inclination in a relationship, where it is often crucial that conflict is acknowledged and dealt with.

THE YOUNGEST CHILD: BORN INTO AN ONGOING ENTERPRISE

Cheerleader, delegator, a people person, the coddled one, the darling little baby; these people are most likely to stop to smell the flowers and watch the sunset. The youngest often grow up to become successful teachers, counselors, and salespeople.

- Charmer/Cute—fun loving/affectionate/can get away with almost anything by being cute and/or by crying
- Understand people
- Fun loving
- Affectionate
- Persuasive
- Good observation skill
- Great delegators—great at getting other people to do things (good con artists)
- Movers of people/manipulators—understand people (know what makes people tick)
- People person—will go with people they feel are the best fit
- Great organizers—skilled at organizing people
- Social—like to party—easygoing personality
- Cheerleaders
- Innovative ideas/creative thinking—come up with craziest ideas
- Possess a different way of looking at life
- Creative problem solvers (conform less often)

- Good intuitive instincts about people and relationships (and are usually right/they should trust their instincts)

The youngest child is most likely to ask, "Why?" This ability to view issues from a critical perspective means they conform less and often come up with creative solutions to problems. One potential drawback is that there are so many people in their lives, they can expect others to take the responsibility for them. The youngest child is often more outgoing and social, and they will usually take risks, meaning that they may get to experience more diverse opportunities (similar to the middle child). The baby of the family often is given an extra dose of affection and attention, as well as dispensation from rules. (Seasoned parents know how fast childhood goes by, so they often tell themselves, let's enjoy this one as long as we can—they are the last proof of the parents' virility). On the negative side, the endless fawning and praise received by these youngsters—primarily because of their place in the family—may leave them feeling that their families do not take them seriously. Additionally, they grow up being coddled one minute as the little darling baby, and the next minute being compared unfavorably with an older sibling. Additionally, they are compared with older siblings (Mr./Miss Wonderful or told that they are the parents' last hope for a successful child). It leaves them teetering between self-confidence and insecurity.

Relationships

The youngest child offers fun and excitement. Whether on a first date or in a serious relationship, you can count on a youngest child to find spontaneous, unexpected ways to ramp up the excitement. This spontaneity can lead to potential problems in a relationship since it may not always be accompanied by dependency and accountability. The lastborns hold powerful social skills that can bring all kinds of rewards, but the youngest children need to be careful not to abuse those powers by manipulating to get what they want.

Innate strengths

Lastborns generally aren't the strongest or smartest in the room, so they develop their own ways of winning attention. They are natural charmers with outgoing, social personalities; no surprise then that many famous actors and comedians are the baby of the family (Stephen Colbert is the youngest of 11), or that they score higher in agreeableness on personality tests than firstborns, according to Sulloway.

Youngest usually end up in the spotlight with their adventurousness. Free-spirited lastborns are more open to unconventional experiences and taking physical risks than their siblings (research shows that they are more likely to play sports like football and soccer than their older siblings, who preferred activities like track and tennis).

Having learned that, as the baby, they cannot insist on anything, some have learned to cajole and beg very effectively—sometimes through smiles, sometimes through tears. The effect is the same: they get what they want.

Common Challenges

Youngest are known for feelings that "nothing I do is important," according to Lerman. "None of their accomplishments seem original. Their siblings have already learned to talk, walk, read, and ride a bike. So parents react with less spontaneous joy at their accomplishments and may even wonder, 'Why can't he or she catch up faster?'"

Lastborns learn to use their role as the baby to manipulate others in order to get their way. "They are least likely to be disciplined," according to Lerman. Parents often coddle the littlest when it comes to chores and rules, failing to hold them to the same standards as their siblings. Parents see the youngest as carefree … and they expect more from their oldest.

As the youngest, lastborns may be introduced by parents as "our baby" even as adults. It is important that lastborns are given the space to grow up.

Necessary Nurturing

Be careful not to allow your youngest to become too dependent on others—that could lead to their being unprepared for the world. Since many babies are seen as too little to participate in chores, they become masters at getting out of work. Keep consistent rules that all the children must follow.

THE ONLY CHILD

Only children learn people skills from parents/peers; most grow up to be movers and shakers, with similar traits as firstborns.

- Ambitious
- Articulate
- Good communicators: get lots of practice being in relationships with adults/peers
- Mature: comfortable interaction with adults; downside: difficulty relating to kids their own age
- Sensitive
- Aloof—never needed to share with siblings
- Never had to share parents
- Confident: used to having adults watch/observe/judge them
- No competition
- Never experience sibling rivalry
- Self-assured
- Serious, like firstborns
- Dependable, like firstborns
- Approach things in an organized way (like firstborns)
- Perfectionist (may be a problem for a partner who is the youngest)
- Willing to sacrifice for other people they care about
- Proceed slowly; are cautious and matter-of-fact (definite strengths resulting from no sibling competition, there is time to think things through)

Innate Strengths

An only child is much like a firstborn, except that he or she never had to share the parents or got to experience the conflict and connection that exist between siblings. Only children are often mature, can be aloof, expecting to receive special treatment/attention from those around them. As children, they are usually serious and dependable, and like the oldest child, they often find great success in school and career.

Only children have wonderful relationship skills. They are dependable and sensitive, and generally will go out of their way for people they care about. They are very good communicators for having lived alone with their parents since birth; they have a lot of practice at being in relationships with adults. Additionally, they need to relate to their peers for play and school. The only child seems to possess the competencies of the Emotionally Intelligent.

Common Challenges

Perfectionism is one trait that an only child needs to watch out for; this can present a real challenge to a partner, especially if that partner happens to be a youngest child. Another issue for onlys to remain aware of is the tendency to proceed slowly. Their caution and laidback approach are definite strengths in much of their lives. But there may be times when they need to step out a bit more and take some risks that allow a relationship to move forward and grow deeper. Additionally, only children tend to be hypochondriacs more often than those with siblings are (parents can dote more when there is a hint of an illness).

Necessary Nurturing

The only child, like firstborns, constantly receives encouragement for their achievements. Most onlys are achievers and can successfully relate with adults; be sure the only child spends time on the playground, on sports teams, and at other organized activities with peers, cousins, and friends.

DOUBLE HAPPINESS: TWINS (AND OTHER MULTIPLES)

Even if they have other siblings, twins (and other multiples) generally grow up as an entity unto themselves—because that is how others tend to see them. The firstborn twin typically acts as the older child in the twosome while the secondborn will have the traits of a younger sib (see the work of Dr. Kevin Lerman). Outside of their relationship, however, they often get lumped together as "the twins." This can be a source of frustration when twins get older and each seeks to carve out an individual identity. So encourage your duo to develop their own passions. While they might prefer to do things together, it is important for each child to establish his or her own interests and personality.

CONCLUSION

It is important to note that birth order can affect ambitions. The famed psychologist Alfred Adler was one of the first people to propose that there was some sort of correlation between our personalities and our position in the family. Birth order has been studied as far back as the 1800s; however, we don't often realize just how much it can affect our relationships and how we deal with people in our everyday lives. When we look at birth order, we often see similar traits and characteristics in terms of where one falls in the family line-up. According to research, firstborn children tend to be extremely ambitious. They possess a very high level of drive and determination. They are also known for perfectionism, which is a double-edged sword because for as positive as that can be, perfectionists can be very critical of themselves. Only children are the most similar to the eldest children; however, they tend not to do as well socially when they are younger, but this seems to change as they get older and are exposed to more social settings and learn to adapt to the environment around them. Middle children seem to be very competitive and innovative. That innovation makes them stand out from their siblings, which they often yearn for. They also make great negotiators. The youngest children really seem to thrive socially because from a very young age, older family members nurture them. They also may reach some major milestones earlier in their lives because they had their older siblings guiding the way. The research indicates that there are many circumstantial factors that come into play when examining birth order but it is also evident that it makes a big impact on how we navigate the life course and on who we become as we age (McGibboney, and Ian. [2014, Jul 06]. "Birth Order Can Affect Ambitions," *Reno Gazette*).

Birth order—along with gender, temperament, social class, ethnic background, and parental influence—is certainly a contributing factor in a youngster's personality, but it is important to focus on each individual's character traits. Remember each person is special.

NOTE

1. Fitzpatrick, M. A., and D. M. Badzinski (1994). "All in the Family: Interpersonal Communication in Kin Relationships." In M. L. Knapp and G. R. Miller (eds.), *Handbook of Interpersonal Communication* (2nd ed.) 726–771. CA: Sage.

UNIT FOUR

SOCIAL COMPETENCIES AND RESOLVING CONFLICTS

DEFINE THE FIVE STRATEGIES/TECHNIQUES FOR MANAGING CONFLICT AND THE APPROPRIATENESS OF EACH

By Benita Bruster, Austin Peay State University

WHAT ARE SOME PRODUCTIVE AND UNPRODUCTIVE WAYS TO MANAGE CONFLICT?
WHAT ARE THE FIVE MOST COMMON STRATEGIES OR TECHNIQUES I CAN LEARN THAT WILL HELP ME RESOLVE OR MANAGE CONFLICT EFFECTIVELY?
SOME PRODUCTIVE AND UNPRODUCTIVE WAYS TO MANAGE CONFLICT

Conflict management is the ability to work through points of contention effectively and fairly. We all know that conflict is an inevitable result of not being able to deal effectively with issues or people in uncomfortable situations. According to Bodine, R.J., Crawford, D.K., and Schrumpf, F. (1994), conflict is a part of life. Without conflict, there is no personal growth or social change. From time to time everyone finds themselves in situations where conflicts arise. Hardin (2012) stated that conflicts may result from a multitude of reasons. Some motives for conflict are much more difficult to resolve than others, such as conflicts about beliefs or principles. It is not a question of whether you *will* encounter conflict, but *when* and *with whom* it will occur. There are many ways to deal with conflict. We all know some productive ways to manage conflict and some strategies for managing conflict that probably will not result in positive outcomes. In order to be a productive contributing citizen, conflict management is an essential skill. There are opportunities to manage conflict in all parts of your personal and professional life. This section of the book outlines five strategies that are most widely used to manage conflict effectively. There are advantages and disadvantages to each of the five strategies; therefore, it is essential that you understand and can selectively apply the strategy that appropriately addresses the specific nature of your conflict. The five strategies for managing conflict:

1. *Avoiding*: We all have people, places, things, and tasks that we avoid. What are the times in your life that you choose to avoid certain people or events in order to stay out of conflict?
2. *Accommodating*: Accommodating sounds like such a nice word, everyone happy and congenial. Is this always the case? Are there times that you were accommodating to others and you left the situation feeling annoyed or disappointed in yourself?
3. *Compromising*: What a fair-sounding word; however, is *equal* always *fair* to all concerned? Are there times that you used the strategy of compromise and felt that you lost what you really wanted?
4. *Competing*: Not everyone has a competitive spirit, but often there are clear winners and losers. What are your feelings about competition and are you willing to accept being on the losing side?
5. *Collaborating*: What a congenial word! Collaborating is a buzz term that simply means that all opinions, sides, and points of view are heard and considered by all stakeholders, resulting in an agreement between all parties. Have your experiences with collaboration had amenable results?

The model in Fig. 15.1 is based on the one that was developed by Blake and Mouton (1964). This model, the Managerial Grid, is just as applicable to our lives today as it was in 1964, more

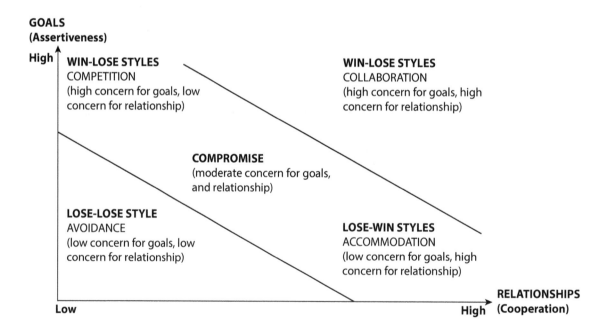

Fig. 15.1 Framework of Five Conflict Strategies

Fig. 15.2 Young/Old Woman

William Ely Hill / Copyright in the Public Domain.

than 50 years later. This framework clearly details the benefits and risks associated with each of the five strategies. In a situation of conflict, you must be able to clearly access your goals or desires as a result of conflict. The relationships with the people affected by this conflict may change based on the conflict. You might ask yourself, "Is the juice worth the squeeze?" "What do I have to win or lose?" and "How will the relationships with others be affected?" Many times conflict can be managed by understanding the perceptions of others. An activity to understand how perceptions can positively or negatively affect others may help bridge differences and help to avoid conflict. This activity will aid in building inclusion to a group and will influence how individuals communicate with others. Below is an activity that deals with perceptions and the transmission of information.

OBJECTIVES

1. To promote inclusion and influence
2. To promote an understanding of different points of view
3. To demonstrate how perceptual limitations can affect communication

INSTRUCTIONS

1. Have the individuals or small groups of three to five meet.
2. Hand out copies of the young girl/old woman drawing to each individual or small group. Instruct individuals to glance at the drawings briefly, without discussion. Then collect all copies immediately.
3. Share what you see in the drawing. Remember, we all perceive things differently; ask questions to your group members, such as "Would you like to talk to this person on the bus?" or "Who in your family does this person remind you of?"

4. Give out the copies of the drawing to each person again and continue the discussion.
5. Assist anyone who appears to have difficulty identifying both aspects of the drawing.
6. Expand the discussion to other areas focusing on different points of view. Such as, "What are your perceptions?"
7. Discuss this with a friend: "How does limiting the points of view cause narrow perceptions or points of view?" "What do limited perceptions have to do with conflict?"

SUGGESTED REFLECTION QUESTIONS

Content/Thinking (look at Fig. 15.2):

- Why do some of you see a young girl while others see an old woman? Is there a correct way to see the picture?
- Why is this an important activity to do?

Social

- Why do conflicts arise between individuals who perceive information differently?
- How can you resolve conflicts based on different perceptions?

Personal

- What did you feel toward the students who saw the drawing the same way you did/differently than you did?
- How did you feel when you "discovered" the other aspect of the drawing?

Appreciation

- Invite statements of appreciation:
- "I am a lot like you when..."
- "I felt good when you said..."

This perception and transmission of information is an excellent activity to use when trying to help individuals to understand the importance of seeing both sides of an issue or to broaden or change perceptions. On many occasions, conflict may be avoided altogether when perceptions change. However, because this is not always the case and conflict is inevitable, having strategies that help understand conflict is essential.

Conflicts emerge among friends, co-workers, partners, children, and parents; conflict is a part of almost every relationship. Understanding how to identify conflict, how to respond to conflict, and how to develop constructive ways to resolve conflict are essential to reaching agreeable solutions. This is an important step in building and maintaining healthy relationships. Arming yourself with information on strategies to identify how to deal with conflict is one vital step to resolving conflict. There are five identified strategies helpful in identifying and resolving conflict. These strategies will help you make informed and thoughtful decisions when conflicts arise.

The five strategies are:

1. Accommodating: Lose-win style
2. Avoiding: Lose-lose style
3. Collaborating: Win-win style
4. Competing: Win-lose style
5. Compromising: Lose-lose and win-win styles

Accommodation as a strategy: *Accommodating the needs of the other person – Lose-win – The person who is accommodated wins while the other side loses*

Accommodation occurs when individuals cooperate at a higher level. An accommodating individual makes the decision to relinquish his or her personal or professional goals, accept less than was expected, or change perspectives. That individual's goals, objectives, and desired outcomes are set aside.

Positive Outcomes for This Strategy

Accommodation produces surface harmony and builds goodwill. It avoids disruption and usually results in the user being seen as a reasonable person and good relations are maintained with the other person.

Negative Outcomes for This Strategy

Accommodation could result in resentment, defensiveness, and possible sabotage if issues remain suppressed. The source of conflict rarely goes away. This strategy can create feelings of losing and lack of influence and recognition for the person who does the accommodating. Generally, there is low commitment to a solution.

Accommodation Is Appropriate to Use When
- Preserving harmony and avoiding disruption are especially important
- One person has a great deal more power than the other

- It is more important to preserve a relationship than to deal with an insignificant issue through conflict
- The conflict issue is more important to the other person
- It is advantageous to allow the other person to experience winning
- Using this style may make the other person more receptive on a more important issue
- Thorough exploration of issues is needed

Accommodation Is Inappropriate to Use When

- Reluctance to deal with conflict leads to evasion of an important issue
- Others are ready and willing to deal with an issue
- Each side has very strong needs and concerns in the situation
- Commitment to the solution is required

Applied Accommodating Exercise
The "What did you decide..."
Think of an example in your personal life when you were accommodating.
What did you decide to relinquish?

1. Discuss this with a classmate.
2. How did you feel after the event or activity?
3. If you had the opportunity to change the outcome, would you?
4. Are you satisfied with the results?

Avoiding as a strategy: *Avoiding the conflict—Lose-lose—Both sides in the conflict lose if the conflict is not addressed later on*

Avoiding the conflict: In many situations, you may think avoiding the conflict is the best way to resolve it. You may be thinking, if I just avoid this person, topic, or situation, the problem may go away. But we all know this is usually not the case. The strategy is considered a lose/lose result; both parties will ultimately lose in terms of goals and relationships. Avoiding is an attempt to resolve the conflict; however, this type of resolution does not help anyone reach goals or resolution. Avoiding, many times, ends in a temporary relief and results in a loss for most involved. As soon as you are in the presence of the other person in this lose/lose scenario, the conflict will return because the problem remains unresolved.

Positive Outcomes for This Strategy

Avoidance allows for a cool-down period. It provides time to get additional information and/or make an analysis of the situation. This strategy avoids stirring up hostilities and hurting the feelings of others. It prevents the individual from being overwhelmed by the conflict in progress.

Negative Outcomes for This Strategy

Avoiding the conflict allows the problem to remain unresolved and it can blossom into a larger conflict. The needs of the parties from both sides are not met. It can result in low commitment to resolving the conflict and poor implementation of any decisions that may have been reached.

Avoidance Is Appropriate to Use When

- There is little chance for a win on either side
- Confronting benefits are overshadowed by potential damage
- Timing is wrong
- A cooling-off period is needed
- There is not enough time to come to resolution
- Others could resolve the conflict more easily
- The problem is viewed as a symptom of a more extensive problem that must be dealt with later

Avoidance Is Inappropriate to Use When

- Viewed as a permanent strategy
- The issue is important
- The issue will not disappear but build to unmanageable proportions
- There is no need to take a position
- Thorough exploration of issues is required
- User's behavior will be viewed as indifference

Applied Avoidance Exercise

Avoidance is certainly one strategy that we all have used to deal with conflict. Think about a time that you used avoidance as a way to deal with conflict and complete this activity.

- Close your eyes and visualize the situation that you avoided.
- What types of emotions are you feeling?
- Use a piece of paper and draw the scenario where you used avoidance.

- Share your drawing with a peer and discuss the questions below.
  - How did your situation conclude?
  - Are you pleased with the outcome?
  - Did the avoidance strategy work for this situation?
  - What would you change?

<u>Collaboration as a strategy:</u> *Collaboration—Win-win—A mutually satisfactory agreement is found so both sides walk away winning*

Collaborating individuals become partners or pair up with each other to achieve both of their goals; this breaks out of the win-lose paradigm and may result in a win for both parties.

Positive Outcomes for This Strategy

When collaboration is used as a strategy, the abilities, values, and expertise of everyone involved are recognized. Creative ideas and solutions to complex problems are likely to emerge. Participants feel respected and valued. Participants learn that a conflict issue can make a constructive contribution to the quality of human relationships. This method builds problem-solving skills, develops a high commitment to solutions, and encourages group cohesiveness.

Negative Outcomes for This Strategy

Collaboration requires more time and energy than other methods.

Collaboration Is Appropriate to Use When

- It is essential that the parties be committed to the resolution
- Issues warrant the time and energy required to seek optimal solutions
- Parties are trained in the use of the process or there is time to train the parties how to collaborate
- Long-term solutions are sought
- Goals of both parties are extremely important; strong investments exist
- The resources of time, abilities, and commitment are available

Collaboration Is Inappropriate to Use When

- The issue is insignificant
- Time, abilities, and commitment are not present
- Commitment to solutions is not important

Applied Collaboration Exercise

Collaboration is usually considered a winning strategy for both parties. Collaboration is used when conflict occurs and there is a feeling of wanting to preserve the relationship with the other person. Collaboration is best used when the issue is not as important as the relationship. Take a moment to complete this collaboration exercise.

1. Think about a meaningful relationship.
2. Remember a time that collaboration was used to reach consensus on an issue.
3. What was the conflict?
4. Was conflict avoided?
5. How did you feel after collaboration?
6. Do you think your relationship with the other person was strengthened, weakened, or changed?
7. Was collaboration effective? Why or why not?
8. Share these memories with someone else.

Competition as a strategy: Competitive style—Win-lose—One side will win the argument and the other side will lose

Competing is a win-lose approach. Competing is generally considered a very assertive way to achieve goals without seeking to cooperate with others. Many times competing may be done at the expense of others. Competing is used as a method to settle conflict when the conflict must be resolved right away. Competing is generally considered negative because one party wins and one party loses.

Positive Outcomes for This Strategy

Competing offers protection from those who tend to take advantage of noncompetitive behavior. This method provides quick, decisive action. It sets the course when you know you are right. It saves time.

Negative Outcomes for This Strategy

This method may intimidate or coerce others into conflict. Competition results in win/lose if the dominated party sees no hope for its side. There is a lack of support for outcomes. Feelings of resentment, hostility, helplessness develop. There is a later renewal of settled conflict. The user may not receive important information and feedback from others. The user may be seen as belligerent, and may ultimately be cut off from interaction with others.

Competition Is Appropriate to Use When

- Quick, decisive action is required
- The right way is clear
- Commitment to outcomes is not important and does not cause harm to others
- Approach has been agreed upon
- User has legitimate power
- Other forms of conflict resolution are clearly inappropriate

Competition Is Inappropriate to Use When

- Other forms of handling conflict are clearly appropriate
- Commitment to outcomes is important
- Losers have no way to express needs
- Maintaining positive relationships is important
- Feedback and interaction with others are needed
- Both parties require high satisfaction of needs and wants

Applied Competition Exercise

Competition is a strategy that we have all used. Have you ever played rock, paper, scissors? This is a competitive and usually low-risk form of competition. For the most part, we are all competitive by nature. We live in an extremely competitive society. We compete for grades as students, jobs as adults, and resources for survival—such as food, shelter, water—and gathering the essentials for living. Competition is a way of life for most. How can competition be used effectively as a strategy for resolving conflict? Try the competition exercise below:

- Find a friend/colleague in your class.
- Individually identify a movie that has just been released that you want to watch, or identify your favorite restaurant where you want to eat dinner.
- Discuss the movie or restaurant options with your colleague.
- Agree to decide the conflict by using competition.
- Take out a coin.
- Have the person in the group of two who has the next birthday flip the coin in the air and call heads or tails.
- Declare the winner. Who wins the movie choice or restaurant pick for dinner?
- Discuss the results with your friend/colleague.
- How do you feel as the winner?

- How do you feel as the loser?
- Was a competition an effective strategy for resolving this conflict?
- When is competition an effective approach and when is it probably not the best approach for resolving conflict?

Compromise as a Strategy: Compromising results in a lose-lose scenario; both sides in the conflict will lose and both sides will win something, too.

Compromising results in a lose-lose and win-win scenario where neither person really achieves what they want. This requires a moderate level of assertiveness and cooperation. When a temporary solution is required, or when both sides have equally important and fairly consistent goals, it may be appropriate to compromise.

Positive Outcomes for This Strategy

More total needs are met and more issues are confronted using compromise than through all styles except collaboration. There is a relatively high degree of satisfaction with the solution that is reached. Each side shares in the winning. It develops skills of bargaining and negotiation and builds the ability to make concessions.

Negative Outcomes for This Strategy

Only partial satisfactions of each side's needs are obtained. The user may appear to be weak, lack commitment to a position, put expediency above principle, and/or seek short-term solutions at the expense of long-term objectives. Each shares in losing. Each side may take on an inflated position, thus masking the issues. The solution may be weakened so that it may not be effective. Compromise can produce little real commitment by any of the parties.

Compromise Is Appropriate to Use When

- A conflict is not important enough to either party to warrant the time and psychological investment in one of the more assertive modes of conflict management
- It is the only practical way of handling a conflict situation in which two equally persuasive parties attempt to work out a solution
- Both parties have enough leeway to give
- Resources are limited
- Temporary solutions are sought for complex issues
- Time is short
- Goals of the parties are moderately important but not worth the effort and time required for collaboration

- The parties are strongly committed to mutually exclusive goals and it is unlikely that either party has the power to dominate the other
- Collaborative efforts fail

Compromise Is Inappropriate to Use When

- Original inflated positions are unrealistic
- Commitment to solution is required
- Thorough exploration of issues is needed
- Both parties require high satisfaction of needs and wants

Applied Compromise Exercise

Compromise is best used when both parties have a mutual goal. The key to effective compromise is that each party involved in the compromise situation feels like they were somewhat successful in the resolution and leaves the conflict with partial satisfaction. Individuals who effectively use compromise are skilled at negotiation and bartering.

1. Turn to a friend/colleague and define the terms *negotiate* and *barter*.
2. After discussing the terms' definitions, think of a time that you used compromise as a strategy to resolve conflict.
3. Identify the conflict.
4. Both take out a piece of paper.

Table 15.1: Label Conflict

NEGOTIATING	BARGAINING

1. Draw a T-chart on your paper, similar to the one above. Write *Negotiating* on one side and *Bargaining* on the other side, and label your conflict on the top of the T-chart.
2. Complete the T-chart by listing as many negotiating and bargaining items as you can think of. What did you negotiate for in order to share in the winnings?
3. What were you willing to give up or give in to win?
4. What were your bargaining chips? What do you have of value that you are willing to give up so that you may have a partial win? List these items in the bargaining column.
5. What was the result of the compromise?
6. Were you satisfied with the results of the compromise?
7. Was compromise an effective way to resolve the conflict?

ASSERTIVENESS AND COOPERATION

These five styles for managing conflict differ in the degree of and relationship to assertiveness and cooperation. When choosing an appropriate strategy for managing conflict, it is helpful to consider two key factors:

Assertiveness—the extent to which we attempt to satisfy our own concerns, our goals.
Cooperation—the extent to which we attempt to satisfy the concerns of others, concerns for the relationship.

Understanding the strategies for effectively managing conflict can lead to a constructive way to maintain a peaceful resolution. Evaluate each situation and determine your level of assertiveness and cooperation for each conflict. These two factors will help determine which strategy is appropriate for each situation. The results of conflict can be as extreme as a world war to as inconsequential as which movie to watch on television. Conflict has the potential to be extremely beneficial, as well as explosively harmful. In our personal and professional lives, it is essential that conflict be understood and managed, and strategies considered in order to manage conflicts effectively rather than conflicts resulting in irreversible negative outcomes that may change lives forever.

REFERENCES

Blake, R. R., and Mouton, J. S. (1964). *The Managerial Grid.* Houston: Gulf.

Bodine, R. J., Crawford, D. K., and Schrumpf, F. (1994). *Creating the Peaceful School: A Comprehensive Program for Teaching Conflict Resolution. Program Guide.* Champaign, IL: Research Press.

Hardin, C. J. (2012). *Effective Classroom Management: Models and Strategies for Today's Classroom.* 3rd Ed. 214–229, Pearson Education, Allyn & Bacon, Boston.

Thomas, K. W. (1992). "Conflict and Conflict Management: Reflections and Updates." *Journal of Organizational Behaviors. 13*(3). 265–274.

CHAPTER 16
STRESSFUL CONFLICT—JOURNEY TO SOLUTIONS

By Joey Palermo

HOW CAN WE MANAGE OUR STRESS?

Anyone can become angry, that is easy. But, to be angry with the right person, to the right degree, at the right time, for the right reason and in the right way—this is not easy.

—Aristotle, Nicomachean Ethics

Two men looked out of prison bars; one saw mud and the other saw stars. Then one asked the other, "What, are you blind?" The other answered, "No, I just see things differently."

INTRODUCTION

Conflict and stress (CS) have an intimate relationship, laden with feelings, values, fitness levels, tolerance, and networks. Both conflict and stress are personal and interpersonal, subjective and objective. Both stimulate an alarm reaction and a response, internal and external. This chapter will focus on the yin and yang relationship of conflict and stress, including the related physiological reactions. I will refer to CS levels defined as the type and amount of stress related to intrapersonal (within the self), interpersonal (between individuals), intragroup (within a group), intergroup (between groups) and international (between nations) conflict. CS levels are responses to specific events, such as those related to family, career, or political ideology.

This discussion will refer to CS and offer recommendations from the health sciences and professional stress management literature to empower the reader with resolve. We will refer to long-term established theories and offer specific exercises to ease the cognitive dissonance and thinking tension that happen. We will provide strategies that can give us a chance for our minds and bodies to reply in a healthy *way*. I emphasize "way" purposely, to introduce the notion that CS stimulates a course of reactions and responses that pave the way to wellness or illness. Research on eustress (positive stressors like a promotion) and distress (negative stressors like being fired from a job) reports the physiological response to these events can be the same. However, our psychological response is dependent on other variables ranging from personality, resources, and support systems. Because recent brain research provides us the physiological makeup (structure, function, and chemistry) of our psychological responses, I will describe even our psychological responses embedded in CS as physiological (including our thinking and feeling). In short, in CS our emotions are expressed on our face, in our heart, and in our brain. Conflict stimulates both the tension and opportunity for our individual minds to grow or to blow a fuse.

An exploration of steps to winning or losing a conflict influences the outcome. Our responses to conflict and stress are personal experiences and expressions that can form personalities and character. To grumble and live a frustrated life in relation to CS is our normal, even socially acceptable, response. CS in fact hurts and puts us in an automatic defense mode.

Our responses and attitudes toward CS are initially based where making choices is not an option. I assume people want to grow from life's stressors but that's false optimism. In reality, making choices when experiencing CS is almost impossible. Caught in the heat of the moment, pausing to think about how to respond requires experience and discipline. There are people who by their persona and conditioning curb this instinctual response with developed principles like patience, information, and tolerance. Given high levels of CS, their instinctive needs to survive surface, and their self-control goes straight out the window.

Let's begin by taking a moment to reflect on an event in your life where the CS levels were high because of your reaction (perception and action) and your life took a turn for the better or the worse. For the following exercises to work, it is best to attach meaning and relevance to areas of real-life conflict. Beyond your own experiences, we can easily reflect on everyday conflict in relationships that leads to outcomes ranging from peace treaties to war. The key is what to do when CS is activated. Major stressors are drawn from meaningful and important relationships to tangibles like career, finances, relationships, and health levels.

There is the well-adjusted person who manages stressors that would send another into a mental hospital. He or she is cool, calm, and collected in the heat of conflict. That person has an inner resolve, skill set, and attitude that turn CS into a challenge that can be addressed and modified. However, CS is not a negative or positive force; it stimulates a CS level that propels us to evaluate and rethink those real situations. Our interactive response can sabotage and hurt on the one hand, or engage with communication, vision, optimism, and resolve on the other. Practicing stress prevention exercises is the real solution to the CS in our lives and worth the effort, given the alternative of an instinctive frustrated response. Be encouraged: our instincts are healthy and essential to survival, and our prevention exercises involve stimulating and tempering those instincts so that when CS shows its face, we can turn the frown upside down and move forward to a new way of seeing things.

Let us look at some specific definitions of CS.

The medical definition of conflict focuses on mental struggles resulting from external or internal demands and from incompatible or opposing needs, drives, and wishes.

Stress is defined as the experience of a perceived threat, real or imagined, to one's mental, physical, or spiritual well-being that results from a series of physiological responses and adaptations.

The following informed exercises are designed to minimize and redirect CS to positivity and change our normal response to CS. Most daily practitioners of CS prevention have experienced a dramatic or traumatic life event; however, instead of quitting, warring, or sitting in self-loathing, they take to stress prevention as a healthy life alternative.

The "to-know-yourself" clause refers to your values, goals, interests, skills, and attitudes. In this text, it has been referred to as "self awareness" and "self motivation." It is important to know what moves you in order to gauge your CS experience. Some proven tools to help us know ourselves are preference-type indicators, reflective tests, and related instruments that offer a personal profile (see Chapters 5, 8, and 9 in this text). To journal our life events and scripts, have dialogue with besties and loved ones, coaches and mentors, therapists and those informed as to your modus operandi, is constructive information relevant to understanding our CS levels.

CS imposes itself on our mind and body, at times pulls at our heartstrings and makes us crazy because the events are taken personally. Like an intimate other who's stimulating our innermost sentiments, CS makes our hearts palpitate and sometimes even causes a heart attack. Meditation, visualization, absolution, and amends are also important tools to managing your CS levels productively and proactively (see Chapter 6, Fig. 6.2).

Keep in mind that in addition to the personal competencies of self awareness and self motivation, there are social competencies that need to be focused on (see Chapter 8). It takes two to tango and the importance of understanding how our self interacts with others is essential to reaching healthy CS levels. Maslow's model created a hierarchy to explain how frustration stems from a deprivation of unmet or unsatisfied needs. In short, this leads to inner conflict at work, at school, and in our communities. Our response will vary depending on our connections and social networks. Our need for connection and having a voice in our relationships affects CS levels. Perhaps the success of Facebook in today's society is because it provides a connection to those who have shared our life adventures and social history. For healthy CS levels and responses that are proactive and productive, I will present mental, physical, and spiritual passages and exercises to moderate their accompanying stress.

Now let's look at the glass half full and try to be that shining light in the room. It is okay to address conflict in a proactive and emotionally intelligent way. Let us begin with picking ten of the hundreds of resources. Like any exercise, you will have to move a muscle, maybe even change a thought. Either way, you will experience your healthier self if you apply some or all of the following exercises. These exercises may reduce or prevent both internal and external stressors; the exercises provide ways to best engage conflict, from prevention to action.

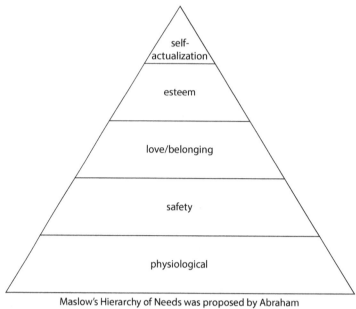

Maslow's Hierarchy of Needs was proposed by Abraham
Maslow in "A Theory of Human Motivation," *Psychological Review*, 1943.

Fig. 16.1 Maslow's Hierarchy of Needs

16.1 APPLIED EXERCISES: TECHNIQUES

The benefits of stress management

Stress management in and of itself is a popular field in behavioral sciences that has found its way into the workplace, the health care industry, and even our prison system. It works and helps to alleviate suffering and minimize violence. Stress management at its best is a tool for inner conflict resolution and peace keeping.

http://www.successfulaging.ca/programs/stress/11.html

The benefits of conflict

Some of our best thinking and creative zeal come from stressful times in our lives. Take a moment to think of conflict in our relationships. Remember the tension, the emotions flaring up, and then the outcome. From the stressful alarm reaction to our body to the repose, there is thinking, debating, and communicating making the conflict a learning experience, good or bad. We can turn deadlines and flat-lines into benchmarks and heartbeats: conflict breeds creativity.

http://www.positivelypresent.com/2011/03/the-upside-of-conflict.html

The benefits of balance and moderation

The importance of mental and physical health when dealing with the daily hassles of life—commuting, work, customers, services, family, health, faith, friends, and technology—must not be understated.

For almost everyone, conflict takes us out of our normal state of mind or emotional balance (homeostasis), threatening our well-being. Before any stressful event, positive or negative, the importance of a quick health quiz can make all the difference in the world in relation to perception, the actual experience, and outcome.

http://www.besthealthmag.ca/best-you/health/quiz-how-healthy-are-you-really

The benefits of balance: tree pose

http://www.everydayhealth.com/healthy-living/how-to-live-a-well-balanced-life.aspx

The benefits of yoga

http://www.everydayhealth.com/fitness-pictures/10-surprising-health-perks-of-yoga.aspx#01

The benefits of knowing your personality

Another influence in how conflict scenarios play out is how our personalities handle issues. Early psychology defined a type-A personality prone to emotional outbursts and self-imposed pressure; the opposite held true for type-B personalities. In addition, how people see you can fuel or shape a conflict challenge. As conflict breeds opportunity, question the tension and your personality.

http://barrysmithconsulting.com/2010/05/05/why-should-i-know-my-presonality-type/

The benefits of affirmations

Our internal stress managers speak to us in the voice of parents, spouses, teachers, preachers, family members, bosses, and strangers. The self-talk in our brain mimics their voices. This inner dialogue creates conflict. For example, you want to marry in ten years; your partner wants to marry now. The internal dialogue of expressed demands in our heads may oppose or impose values in our personal space. Self-talk is at its loudest when experiencing conflict, so why not be aware of what you are saying and phrase your goal clearly, objectively—heck, even passionately?

Affirmations are our inner voice, an extension of heartfelt, sometimes long-term sentiments about issues that pull at our heartstrings and maybe our pockets. Listen to what you are saying and if necessary reconstruct the content so no one is getting hurt. For example, you are speaking with your father about your spendthrift wife. Dad has a way with words that irks you and he's going on and on about how she is going to break your bank and your heart. Your inner voice says, "If he says one more negative thing about my wife, I'm going to punch him in the mouth." Before any further discussion, you can self-affirm, "If he says one more word, I'm going to close my mouth."

http://www.chopra.com/ccl/7-benefits-of-a-daily-affirmation-plan

The benefits of meditation

Conflict breeds opportunity, and the gray area and space where the pedal hits the metal require clarity and focus. This kind of clarity and focus, in the moment of feeling the conflict, takes your breath away. Let us call it a "mindful meditation" where the thinking tension is an experience. That momentary experience usually triggers a deep breath and the pause in between stimulates the brain to open space, gives it a chance to regroup. Meditation, taking time to sit and let your thoughts flow freely or concentrating on a word or image, eases tension and can lull you to sleep.

In conflict, the chance to consciously take stock of your breathing patterns and count to ten or even be conscious of your breathing is liberating and relaxing. No longer does the conflict have to take our breath away, leaving us anxious or agitated—conscious breathing (meditation) turns that tense breath into respiration (a word linked to rejuvenation and health).

http://eocinstitute.org/meditation/meditation-and-breathing-benefits-of-mindful-breathing/

The benefits of letting go and forgiving

Take a piece of paper, write your grievance on it, wad it into a ball, and throw it at the object of your affliction. Did it really go anywhere? Maybe, but it has given us pause. Maybe the professor, the doctor, the pastor, and the enlightened friends were right when they said there's "A blessin' in the lesson and some things can't be explained." My professional work in conflict resolution and as a lecturer on the subject of marriage and family has taught me that relationships are laden with conflict and love sometimes gets a bad rap because it means having to communicate, having to tolerate, and having to understand, and sometimes it means letting go. Forgiveness is in fact forgiving that person and sometimes even yourself (see Fig. 6.2). "This isn't to deny or suppress your emotions. On the contrary, choosing to feel good about letting go actually helps to view and express the person or issue from a much healthier and even loving perspective. You won't dwell upon your grief and sadness, perpetuating it even further; perhaps, your emotions become more balanced as you detach from the drama of it all."

http://www.huffingtonpost.com/pamela-dussault/letting-go-of-relationships_b_1967194.html

The benefits of visualization

I say life and the places we experience daily are like the elements of a moving picture. Shakespeare wrote, "All the world's a stage, and all the men and women merely players." We're dressing up, showing up, and acting up. The grand performance of Life where we are participants in some grand opera where we work, play, laugh, cry, love, lose, and wake up the next day and do it again until we drop... dead. On the way to conflict or conflict as an element of surprise—botched interviews, a flat tire, a jilted lover, a failing grade—can just hit us with a "bam" and alter reality. Either on the way or in the event, how we see it determines our CS level. Every cloud has a silver lining and looking at the glass half full are not only maxims but also tools to turn the sour sweet. Visualization is clearly one of those tools that we can use before, during, and following those life stressors. Close your eyes and imagine a third eye in the center of your forehead where you are the director and CS a moving picture for you to focus, blur, freeze-frame, or Photoshop. Remember, you are the director and this movie is funded and fueled by your imagination. This is the important skill of reframing, critical in successful negotiation and mediation.

http://www.positivethinking-toolbox.com/benefits-of-visualization.html

The benefits of not taking yourself too seriously

"To be nobody but yourself in a world which is doing its best day and night to make you like everyone else is to fight the hardest battle and never stop fighting." e.e. cummings

http://www.pickthebrain.com/blog/why-is-it-so-hard-to-be-yourself/

The benefits of belonging

I am reminded of hearing someone in the next room laughing uncontrollably and mistaking the sound for uncontrollable crying. What is it about our inner self that feels so strongly that conflict and stress become one cry of joy? And from one day to the next the people and things we love change? Perhaps, as some say, we outgrow them, we get tired, or we give up. Or perhaps, there is a power of conscience that stresses us to wake up and make that change toward wellness and self-actualization. Either way, "no man is an island." We need others to share in our life work and awaken the inner voice that responds to stressors and learns from the experience that—good or bad—our conflict and our stress are ours to own up to and accept. So take a deep breath and embrace the journey! Yes, at the end of the day, one of the greatest ironies of our human existence is that the very people, places, and things that stress us to the point of a heart attack can also bring us great joy, again depending on values, perception, expectations, and agreement.

http://www.cnn.com/2012/06/01/health/enayati-importance-of-belonging/

16.2 APPLIED EXERCISE: NATURAL HIGHS

1. Falling in love.
2. Laughing so hard your face hurts.
3. A hot shower.
4. No lines at the supermarket.
5. A special glance.
6. Getting mail.
7. Taking a drive on a pretty road.
8. Hearing your favorite song on the radio.
9. Lying in bed listening to the rain.
10. Hot towels fresh out of the dryer.
11. A chocolate milkshake.
12. A bubble bath.
13. Giggling.
14. A good conversation.
15. The beach.
16. Finding a 20-dollar bill in your coat from last winter.
17. Laughing at yourself.
18. Midnight phone calls that last for hours.
19. Running through sprinklers.
20. Laughing for absolutely no reason at all.
21. Having someone tell you that you're beautiful.
22. Laughing at an inside joke.
23. Friends are angels who lift us to our feet when our wings have trouble remembering how to fly.
24. Accidentally overhearing someone say something nice about you.
25. Waking up and realizing you still have a few hours left to sleep.
26. Your first kiss (either the very first or with a new partner).
27. Making new friends or spending time with old ones.
28. Playing with a puppy.
29. Having someone play with your hair.
30. Sweet dreams.
31. Hot chocolate.
32. Road trips with friends.
33. Swinging on a swing set.
34. Making eye contact with a cute stranger.
35. Making chocolate chip cookies.
36. Having your friends send you homemade cookies.
37. Holding hands with someone you care about.
38. Watching the expression on someone's face as they open a much-desired present from you.
39. Watching the sunrise.
40. Getting out of bed every morning and being grateful for another beautiful day.
41. Knowing that somebody misses you.
42. Getting a hug from someone you care about deeply.
43. Knowing you've done the right thing, no matter what other people think.

16.3 APPLIED EXERCISE: ILLUSTRATION OF CHRONIC STRESS

As we have seen in this chapter, the term "stress" is used in countless ways. It can refer to events or circumstances, such as an examination, that cause us unease; to the general unease we feel during such events; to the specific bodily responses to such events, such as rapid heartbeat; or to the mind's and body's attempts to deal with the unease in order to recapture a sense of wellness. Stress can be defined as a state of imbalance within a person, elicited by an actual or perceived disparity between the environmental demands and the person's capacity to cope with these demands. Stress occurs in response to strain and threatening circumstances in the environment.

The idea of stress has existed for centuries. Hippocrates believed in the humoral theory of illness—that positive health results from a mind and body harmony—perhaps the earliest characterization of an individual who is not stressed out. Hippocrates' belief in the body's self-healing powers is also consistent with an understanding of the body's adaptation to stress. Records indicate that in the fourteenth century, the term was equated with hardship and affliction, and in nineteenth-century medicine, stress was cited as a cause of ill health, as many diseases were attributed by physicians to conditions of melancholia, grief, or despair. Clearly, by the 1800s, there was a clear link between body and mind. Early in the twentieth century, Walter Cannon, an American physiologist, used the term *homeostasis* to describe a state in which the body's physiologic processes are in balance and are properly coordinated. Cannon described a fight-or-flight reaction: when circumstances offered opportunity for success (or there was no other choice), humans would fight; in the face of overwhelming odds, humans sought flight. He described the physiologic changes. Hans Selye, an endocrinologist who is often cited as the classic figure in stress research, said that in our daily lives, we all experience stressful situations. These situations upset our body's equilibrium—our homeostasis—and make us more susceptible to mild diseases and illnesses. If stressful situations persist over an extended period of time, chronic stress, the body's resources become depleted and more severe disease or illnesses—or even death—may result (see the "Chronic stress" section in the Epilogue).

16.4 APPLIED EXERCISE: HAPPINESS/GRATEFULNESS CALENDAR

Every evening as you are falling asleep, during that twilight time between wakefulness and sleep, think about your day. Select one moment or event that made you smile or made you feel grateful. It could be the smallest thing, like hearing a bird sing or seeing a friendly smile. Write this moment down in your calendar. Do this EVERY day.

At the end of the week, look at your daily entries and CIRCLE your weekly winner.

At the end of the month, look at your four weekly CIRCLED entries and select your monthly winner. At the end of the year choose the annual winner from your 12 monthly winners. This will help you to learn to move forward even if it is one baby step at a time.

16.5 APPLIED EXERCISE: MEDITATION AND BEING IN "THE PRESENT"

Set a timer for three minutes. Close your eyes and clear your mind. With your eyes closed, FOCUS on your breathing: exhale to a count of three, inhale to a count of three, and hold your breath for the count of three. Repeat this for three minutes.

CHAPTER 17

BULLYING: DOES IT END WITH HIGH SCHOOL?

By Ilene Rothschild and Howard Miller[1]

Let's start with a quiz. Select the best answer for what a bully is.

a. A fake tough guy who lashes out at those who are smaller or weaker
b. Someone who is insecure and weak
c. Someone who has no sympathy for others
d. Someone who holds a position of power over others
e. Someone who wants to show off in front of others

DISCUSS: What do you think? How would you define what it means to be a bully? Do you agree with any of these answers (culled from a survey of first-year college students), or do you have ideas of your own?

INTRODUCTION

On September 13, 2010, New York Governor Andrew Cuomo signed into law a bill known as the Dignity Act, aimed at helping schools get a firm and consistent grip on what has become a huge public concern for student safety by laying out requirements for handling bullying incidents. Specifically, the law seeks to assure that all elementary and secondary school students are provided "with a safe and supportive environment free from discrimination, intimidation, taunting, harassment, and bullying on school property, a school bus and/or at a school function." The passage of this law—and similar pieces of legislation passed in a majority of states—came on the heels of numerous high-profile and widely publicized incidents in which bullying led to dire consequences; if you are unfamiliar with these, take the time to find out what happened to Phoebe Prince, Rebecca Ann Sedwick, and Tyler Clementi, or learn about school shootings at Columbine High School, Virginia Tech, and

Sandy Hook Elementary School. We are further challenged by pervasive cyberbullying, which can cause significant emotional and psychological distress during or after school hours. So, yes, our awareness has been raised, and we are paying greater attention to these compelling problems. There are numerous books, videos, and movies that address the psychological and social issues involved for the victims as well as the bullies.

HOW DOES BULLYING AFFECT SCHOOL-AGE CHILDREN?

Consider some common scenarios related to bullying:

- A group of popular girls in seventh grade advised others not to eat with a new classmate, Layla. They made fun of her looks, her clothing, her hairstyle, and even her shyness, and because they were popular themselves, the mean girls expected their peers to go along with them.
- A group of teens were mocking another student, Jorge, calling him gay—not based on any knowledge of his sexual orientation, but simply because they decided they didn't like him. When Sam went to support him, the others said, "Oh, you must be gay, too."
- When 16-year-old Aisha was taunted with racial slurs, another student Sheila came to her defense and reported the incident to the school counselor. The counselor praised Sheila for standing up for her friend, but did not consider it of enough importance to do any follow-up. Soon Sheila soon became the target of cyberbullying from the same group of students, who made up ugly lies about her and spread them via social media. They verbally attacked her as well. Eventually, it became unbearable, and Sheila committed suicide.

These examples serve to illustrate that bullying is still a serious issue in schools—despite laws like the Dignity Act—and there are many in positions of responsibility who continue to view it as a normal aspect of childhood.

Bullying is sadly common in the lives of many children and can occur in urban, suburban, small town, or rural settings. As reported by Melton (1998), between 15% and 25% of students are bullied and 15%–20% report bullying others. Some staggering facts, as reported in *Stop Bullying Now* newsletter:

- Victims of bullying have higher rates of depression and anxiety as well as lower self-esteem
- Bullying has been linked with school violence, shootings, and hazing incidents
- Students often report teasing and bullying as a threat to their safety and well-being
- Bullying can be a sign of antisocial and violent tendencies that can lead to delinquency

The good news is that school districts have become more engaged in anti-bullying programs. School or district committees are formed, policies and procedures are agreed upon, and lessons are being developed, all aimed at reducing the number of bullying incidents, increasing awareness, providing support for victims and interventions for the bullies themselves, and teaching bystanders how to respond. Two remarkable anti-bullying programs that can be cited:

1. In Eastchester, New York, a suburban district, Principal Theresa Cherry has established a school-wide program for the elementary school. There is a school motto, "KFC—Kindness Follows Caring." This mantra permeates the environment and is incorporated with activities and events all year. Teachers develop classroom rules, hold welcome-back assemblies, and affirm the themes of civility and kindness. Students are cited for good behavior and the atmosphere reflects this. If bullying occurs, consequences are clear:

    *   Conferences with counselor, principal, and teachers for all
    *   involved parties
    *   Consequences are spelled out, such as recess detention
    *   A reflection journal is required from the bully

    The teachers select books, modify curriculum, and put into place a reward system to emphasize kindness by the students in all school settings. The principal shared one effective community-building lesson: every student writes a kind comment about another student and adds the note as a link to the classroom's paper chain of kindness. An outdoor ceremony is held at the culmination of the year to link the chains from each class to make a school-wide chain. These character education lessons are infused through English and social studies classes and are a common theme of the school: "I'd rather be a buddy, not a bully." It is apparent why this elementary school in Eastchester has won many local and national recognition awards.

2. Another model of an anti-bullying program is the **No Place for Hate** curriculum, sponsored by ADL, the Anti-Defamation League, which is being offered in 1,700 schools across the country. In New Rochelle, New York, a large urban school system has instilled the No Place for Hate (NPH) program in its K–12 schools. NPH was originally established in 1999 and "provides schools and communities with an organizing framework for combating bias, bullying, and hatred, leading to long-term solutions for creating and maintaining a positive climate" (ADL Guide, page 2). Jason Sirois, the National Director for NPH, described the process of how a school becomes an NPH school:

- Each school must officially register with ADL.
- Each school must form an anti-bias committee in the district, including staff members, administrators, parents, faculty, students, and community leaders. Schools may call them Diversity Clubs or Respect Clubs.
- Sign an NPH resolution whereby they commit themselves to a minimum of three anti-bias events that promote respect and recognize differences. Schools are permitted to design community projects tailored to their own school or choose from a project list from ADL.
- Upon successful completion of the projects, the school district is recognized by ADL and designated an NPH school. The school (New Rochelle is a model) receives a banner to commemorate the milestone.

ADL oversees all the nationwide projects of NPH. They provide two facilitators, who have extensive professional training, for each program. Yearly awards are given to celebrities like Lady Gaga, who won a Making a Difference Award for her anti-bullying program, Born This Way.

We have witnessed numerous exemplary programs for anti-bullying and anti-bias initiatives developed each year. Ultimately, incidents of bullying need to be viewed as an opportunity for conflict resolution. Teachers need to intervene (and not ignore) when children's conflicts are about power and control. Intervention, through programs or administrative school action, is appropriate and necessary to prevent or curtail bullying.

DISCUSS: What was bullying like when you were in elementary, middle, or high school? Were you involved in any anti-bullying programs in your schools? What did you learn from the experiences?

HOW DOES BULLYING AFFECT COLLEGE STUDENTS?

Anyone who thinks that bullying ends upon exiting high school is sadly mistaken. In fact, it may worsen, given that college students typically and suddenly find themselves with a great deal of independence, along with unstructured, unsupervised time that frequently is not devoted to their studies. They often discover they have easy access to alcohol and drugs. Temptation plus peer encouragement can lead to the kind of bullying that takes place in the form of rituals like the hazing that sometimes goes on in fraternities, on sports teams, and within military programs on college campuses. This can have dire consequences. Just ask the five fraternity members from the Baruch College chapter of Pi Delta Psi who are about to go on trial, charged with murder in the death of Chun Hsien Deng. Mr. Deng died during a hazing ritual in 2013 during which, according to published reports, he was "blindfolded and forced to wear a backpack weighted with sand while taking blows from fraternity members" (Rojas, 2015). These same students waited a full hour before calling for medical assistance. Mr. Deng later died in the hospital.

Other forms of bullying, including sexual harassment and assaults, are of great concern on college campuses, where students are in an unfamiliar environment, surrounded by lots of strangers about whom they know little or nothing. Key findings from a recent survey of more than 150,000 college students across 27 different campuses in the United States (Association of American Universities, 2015):

- 11.7% of respondents reported having been subjected to nonconsensual sexual contact by physical force, threats of physical force, or incapacitation (i.e., passed out, asleep, or under the influence of alcohol or drugs).
- Undergraduate students identifying as transgender, genderqueer, nonconforming, or questioning (TGNQ) were victims at a higher overall rate of 12.4%.

Two significant findings for serious consideration:
- Only about one fourth of even the most serious incidents were reported to someone in authority.
- Slightly less than half of those surveyed said they witnessed a drunken person heading for a sexual encounter, and most of them said they failed to intervene.

DISCUSS: These two findings are disturbing, but not necessarily surprising. Why do you think most incidents are not reported to someone in authority? Why do you think people generally fail to intervene when their peers are obviously headed for trouble?

Cyberbullying is also a serious concern on college campuses. A study by two Indiana State University faculty members (MacDonald and Robert-Pittman 2010) focused on a much smaller population of 439 college students, but looked specifically at the phenomenon of cyberbullying, a form of bullying that is exacerbated by its ability to mask the identity of the bully. The requirement of no physical effort beyond that needed to post a message on a social media site places the cyberbully in a unique position of power to act on a whim, a sense of revenge, a burst of jealousy, or for any other reason or no reason at all. Those surveyed were presented with this definition of cyberbullying: "sending or posting harmful or cruel text or images using the Internet or other digital communication devices," a definition the researchers culled from the website cyberbully.org. The results of the survey showed that 21.9% had been cyberbullied at college, 38% knew someone who had been cyberbullied, and 8.6% admitted they had cyberbullied others.

WHAT TO DO IN A COLLEGE SETTING

Begin by being proactive. Determine the college's policies regarding bullying, cyberbullying, sexual harassment, and other safety issues, and find out what services the college offers to its students. Work through the Student Government Association, the fraternity/sorority system, or other student-centered organizations to make sure that this information is widely understood and disseminated. Faculty organizations like the Senate can also be your ally in this.

If you are being bullied, find someone to talk to, whether it is one of the college's support services, a friend, the dorm's resident advisor, a faculty member or academic advisor, a college's counselor—someone. You may need help, and a good place to begin is by talking with someone who is not personally tied to the situation. In addition, retain all records of the bullying and determine whether there were witnesses who will back you up if you need to report it.

If someone confides in you, be supportive, listen carefully, consider whether the person might need the help of the college's professional services, and advise accordingly. Be prepared to seek additional advice yourself if you believe the individual is in any danger of harm, including self-inflicted harm.

Remember these words from Elie Wiesel, recipient of the 1986 Nobel Peace Prize: "Silence encourages the tormentor, never the tormented." The opposite of silence is not necessarily confrontation, and certainly you need to consider the situation before stepping in, but think carefully the next time you are in a situation where you can be of assistance to someone. Will you be a bystander or an upstander?

DISCUSS: What do Elie Wiesel's words mean to you? Are there actions you would be willing to take in a situation where you are witness to or have knowledge of any form of bullying?

Define the following terms:
BIAS
BULLY
BULLYING
BYSTANDER
CYBERBULLYING
SOCIAL JUSTICE
UPSTANDER
VICTIM

REFERENCES

Association of American Universities (2015). "AAU Campus Survey on Sexual Assault and Sexual Misconduct." Downloaded October 23, 2015 from http://www.aau.edu/uploadedFiles/AAU_Publications/AAU_Reports/Sexual_Assault_Campus_Survey/AAU%20Campus%20Climate%20Survey%20Full%20Executive%20Summary.pdf

Bazelon, E. (2013). *Sticks and Stones: Defeating the Culture of Bullying and Rediscovering the Power of Character and Empathy*, Random House, New York.

Coloroso, B. (2011). "Bully, Bullied, Bystander... and Beyond." *Teaching Tolerance*. Number 39.

Hirshey, G. (2007). "Pushing Back at Bullying." *The New York Times*, January 28.

Matthiessen, C. (2015). "How to Start an Anti-Bullying Program." Downloaded October 23, 2015 from http//www.greatschools.org/parenting/bullying/slideshows

MacDonald, C. and Robert-Pittman, B. (2010). "Cyberbullying among College Students: Prevalence and Demographic Differences." *Procedia—Social and Behavioral Sciences 9*, 2003–2009.

Miller, H. and Rothschild, I. (2014). "Keeping Your Middle School Child Safe from Bullying." *Journal News*, November 9, 2014.

No Place for Hate (2013). Anti-Defamation League.

Rojas, Rick. "5 Facing Murder Charges in Baruch Hazing Death Appear in Court." *The New York Times*, October 22, 2015.

Rose, C. et al. (2012). *Bullying and Students with Disabilities: The Untold Story Narrative*. Love Publishing Company.

Scarpaci, R. (2006). "Bullying: Effective Strategies for Its Prevention." *Kappa Delta Pi Record, Vol. 42*, Issue 4.

Schargel, F. (2013). "Bullying: What Schools, Parents, and Students Can Do." *The Huffington Post*.

NOTE

1. Dr. Ilene Rothschild is associate professor of special education at Mercy College, Dobbs Ferry, New York. Dr. Howard Miller is professor and chair of the department of secondary education at Mercy College, Dobbs Ferry, New York. Both are certified DASA training providers.

CHAPTER 18

WHAT IS NEGOTIATION? WHAT IS MEDIATION?

By Art Lerman and Nancy Friedman

NEGOTIATION AND MEDIATION

DEFINITIONS AND CAVEATS

Negotiation is a discussion aiming for an outcome that all discussants, the negotiators, will agree upon, often a way to find a mutually acceptable solution to a conflict.

Mediation is a negotiation aided by one or more outside parties; a mediator or mediators who guide the process.

Some would add that mediators should be impartial and disinterested concerning the discussion's outcomes. This, however, would leave many instances of aided negotiation out of the definition of mediation. It may be an ideal to have mediators impartial and disinterested in the discussion's outcomes, but in many instances, mediators promote their view of the best outcomes—for the negotiators themselves, for the society in which the negotiators live, and/or for the mediators' self-interests. It should be acknowledged that interested mediator involvement can, in some cases, weaken a sense of empowerment for the parties, as they do not feel they own the outcome, the resolution, because the mediator then has a hand in it.

Mediators, for example, may work for a solution that is good not only for two disputing neighbors, but also for their neighborhood. In international relations, it's typical for a nation to mediate a dispute between its allies—to unify an alliance that strengthens the international position of the mediating nation itself.

Yes, there is a point in which the mediators' promotion of their own preferences crosses a boundary, and they become just one more of the negotiating parties.

And there is another boundary. At the point the aiding parties may be powerful enough to determine the outcomes at which the negotiators arrive, it is no longer negotiation or mediation. It is arbitration or adjudication—processes in which outcomes are determined, not by negotiators, but by outside authorities.

It is a matter of empowerment. By definition, negotiation and mediation empower negotiators to decide their own fate concerning the matter under discussion.

NEGOTIATION/MEDIATION AND SKILL

Power is effective only if the empowered have the skill to use it. So another necessary element in the mix is skill. Negotiators must have the skill to use their power to come to a mutually agreeable outcome.

Negotiating power, therefore, is not simply a matter of control to obtain one's preferred outcomes. It's the ability to work with others to forge outcomes preferred by all negotiators. Instead of the more typical view of power, power *over*, it's a much more difficult kind of power: power *with*.

In mediation, it's the mediator's job to help build these skills if they are not sufficiently available to the negotiators.

Mary Parker Follett (1868–1933), a major American thinker on democracy and social organization, introduced the notion that, even though power is usually understood as power over others, it is also possible to view power as power with others. In this way, a more collaborative, less coercive dynamic is fostered. (Morton Deutsch, Peter T. Coleman, Eric C. Marcus, eds, *The Handbook of Conflict Resolution* [2nd Ed.; San Francisco: Wiley/Jossey-Bass, 2006]).

Internationally, soft power (building on trustworthiness, empathy, values, etc.) as opposed to hard power (using military might, coercive economic sanctions, etc.) has been used to turn the tide and bring resolution to conflicts. Hard power may gain a temporary win, but often creates even more resistance in the future, whereas soft power creates the potential for long-lasting positive change.

NEGOTIATION/MEDIATION: THE SKILLS OF DEMOCRACY

Thus, in terms of society at large, mediation and negotiation are central to democracy. Participants themselves, not outside authorities, make the decisions. Mediation and negotiation training is training in democracy—in democratic citizenship.

Crossing the boundary into arbitration and adjudication, where parties either stop negotiating or decide from the onset not to negotiate (instead allowing others to decide for them), is, at least for the particular decision involved, a ceding to authoritarianism—something that those who value democracy, their own empowerment, must be very careful not to overdo.

In the Western philosophical tradition, it was Thomas Hobbes (1588–1679) who argued that people do not have the negotiation abilities to decide for themselves. Hobbes' only alternative was to cede decision-making powers to others.

John Locke (1632–1704) took a more optimistic view. Reflecting the movement away from Hobbesian-justified authoritarianism, Locke argued that people did have the mediation and negotiation abilities to make their own decisions. Locke's thinking therefore is found to be instrumental in the development of democratic thought—as in the early documents of the American Revolution. Some argue that crime and interpersonal violence in London decreased between Hobbes and Locke, easing Locke into a more optimistic view of negotiators' abilities.

This optimism continues on in the ethos of today's negotiation/mediation trainers. In the words of Dr. Stephen Slate, executive director and principal trainer for the Bronx-based Institute for Mediation and Conflict Resolution, "People have what it takes to make a difference in their lives." Or, in the very optimistic words of Titus Rich, the Institute's Director of Mediation, "Just give a solid introduction to the mediation process and get out of the way."

As mediators we have been impressed by the capabilities of the parties to come to mutually satisfying outcomes. There are even times when all the mediators and mediator centers do is to provide safe and comfortable places for this to take place.

NEGOTIATION/MEDIATION SKILLS

So what are the skills? The other sections/chapters of this volume are a solid reference. One finds negotiation and mediation skills in the sections on the six C's, the feelings wheel, open communication, emotional intelligence, empathy, paraphrasing, reframing, nonverbal communication, active listening, anger management, and recognizing different types of conversations.

The skills are described in this volume and in parallel works on negotiation and mediation. They are there to be studied and learned. In actual negotiations and mediations, the negotiators may already be familiar with them.

Accessing the Skills' Focal Points

The issue is, with so many skills/techniques, how does one access them in the heat, excitement, and emotional flutter of the negotiation/mediation moment?

One strategy is to focus on just a few central points that one can keep in mind (or on a note pad you keep handy) even during stress. And, with familiarity and practice, the mind may take these points as portals to the plethora of other relevant skills such as are shown in this volume. An allied strategy is to have a co-mediator to help keep the central points in focus, and to use them as portals to the larger universe of helpful skills.

Two Skill Sets: The Competitive Set

So, can we now turn to presenting these focal skills?

Not quite. There is another boundary to be recognized. There are two sets of focal skills, depending on the goals of negotiators.

There are two types of negotiating goals—the competitive and the collaborative—each implying a different set of skills. Much of the above discussion, and most of the skills in this volume, are based on a collaborative approach—negotiators searching for mutual benefit. Yet, there is a very popular literature about competitive negotiation: each side seeking its own goals, caring little for or even striving to undermine the other side's goals. (See "win-lose," Chapter 16 of this volume.)

This volume and this section are dedicated to the collaborative skill set. But since this section is here to introduce negotiation and mediation generally, a competitive negotiation skill set deserves a few words.

The first word is that there is much overlap between the two sets of skills. Competitive negotiators do well to study collaborative skills, since they are designed to fully understand and relate to those on the other side. The difference is that the understanding and relating are used to narrower and more self-serving ends by competitive negotiators.

And these ends are bolstered by specifically competitive skills that the competitive negotiator stands ready to use as opportunities appear. Here are a few archetypical examples:[1]

- Good Cop/Bad Cop: One negotiating partner presents him- or herself as very difficult and threatening. When he or she steps out of the room, the remaining partner suggests a quick deal with the other side, to mollify the difficult partner and keep the situation from getting out of hand.
- Highball/Lowball: The competitive negotiators start off with an offer way too high or too low, throwing the other parties off balance, drawing them further toward the competitors' favored position.
- Bogey: The competitors heavily defend a position that they really do not care about, finally giving it up and expecting the other side to make a sacrifice of something really important in return.
- The Nibble: After long and hard bargaining, with an agreement finally on the table ready for signature, the competitors suggest throwing in a small extra for their side, putting all the hard work in jeopardy if the other side does not simply say okay.
- Chicken: "I'm coming at you in my truck. I just threw the steering wheel and the brake pedal out the window. You'd better swerve."
- Legitimacy: We have the expertise and know your interests better than you do.

A final word about the competitive approach: No one likes to lose. If one feels he or she has lost in a competitive negotiation, resentment, regret, and a desire for revenge are likely to ensue. The agreement, whatever it was, will be in danger of collapsing.

Even for the winners, their reputation may make it difficult to find others in the future willing to deal with them.

The Collaborative Skill-Set Focal Points

So we return to the collaborative, win-win negotiation approach (also Chapter 16), which takes into consideration the needs of all parties and promises better outcomes in the long run for oneself and for others.

Here, there is a chance for better understanding of varying perspectives, and the opportunity to develop trust among parties. Therefore, this has been called a transformative approach, as it has the potential for transforming individuals, communities, and society as a whole. In a negotiation or mediation session, the collaborative approach recommends three sets of points to focus on.

The first is to keep in mind that in all negotiation/mediation sessions, one is dealing with forces that come from three social levels:[2]

- The individual level—the psychology of the parties involved.
  - The particularity of each party's psychology—on the immediate issue, on such issues generally, and on human relationships overall—will always be relevant.
- The social group level—patterns of interaction between the individuals involved.
  - Individuals are always enmeshed, entangled, in all sorts of interpersonal configurations, strongly influencing—perhaps constraining, perhaps liberating—their ability to analyze and plan creatively.
- The overarching societal context, within which the individuals and their interactions take place.
  - Individuals and their interpersonal groups exist in the larger social contexts of economic/social class, religion, ethnicity, gender, and age differences, which further constrain or liberate their analytical and planning abilities.

Second, when individuals bring the forces emanating from these levels into the negotiation/mediation room, there are eight central recommendations for their discussion for describing, analyzing, planning:[3]

- Parties should patiently listen to each other.
- Listening should be followed up by checking understanding by restating what the other has said.

- Delve into what each person says by exploring the fundamental interests/needs that motivate stated positions.
- Reframe the disagreement as a problem shared by both parties (i.e., figuratively or actually sit on the same side of the table and face the problem as a united problem-solving team).
- Honor multiple perspectives.
- Develop awareness of self and of others.
- Create space for alternative ways of interpreting interactions.
- Focus on effective communication (active listening; listening to understand; asking questions that allow for deeper, more thorough sharing and understanding).

Third, while attending to this more or less intellectual task of description, analysis, and planning, keep in mind that the matter is not just about concrete facts to be listed, ordered, and reordered. The facts are infused with emotions, and the parties discussing these facts are emotional. So for an in-depth understanding of the facts, and for the parties to effectively discuss them, points about emotions should also be kept in mind.[4]

- Appreciation: Try to have all parties feel appreciated.
- Affiliation: Parties should feel some connection to each other.
- Autonomy: Parties should feel a measure of control over their situation (ACBD: Always Consult Before Deciding).
- Status: Each party should feel respected for his or her experience and expertise.
- Role: In the discussion and in the outcome, each party should feel it has a fulfilling role.

Concluding: These three sets of guidelines—concerning levels, discussion, and emotion—are central for negotiators and mediators. They are the frame for keeping sessions on track, and portals for bringing in other skills/ideas for negotiation and mediation, as noted in this volume and in the vast negotiation/mediation literature generally.

Mechanics of the Mediation Process

The collaborative skills introduced here are central to negotiation and mediation. What is special about mediation is that it is for the mediators to bring collaborative skills to negotiations when called for. This can be done by direct teaching and by modeling. Two areas of more direct teaching are the introductory statement, in which the mediator explains the mediation process to the parties, and then when the mediator structures the ensuing discussion.

Following is an introduction to each of these processes.[5]

Mechanics of the Mediation Process: The Introduction[6]

1. Preparing the room: Formal business or living room type of environment, depending on nature of situation and available facilities.
2. Questions: Mediators ask parties if they have any questions about the foregoing.
3. Begin: Mediation commences. (See following.)

Following is an introduction to each of these processes.

Mechanics of the Mediation Process: The Introduction

- Preparing the Room
  - Formal business or living room type of environment—depending on nature of situation and available facilities.
- Physical Safety: Avoid anything that can be used as a weapon.
  - Writing materials—felt-tip (safe) pens, paper, and/or computer for note taking and agreement writing.
  - Places for everyone, with some distance between opposing parties (opposing parties facing one another), and places for mediators (near the door) and, if necessary, observers and/or translators.
- Greeting Parties
  - Greet parties outside of the room, exchange pleasantries, and usher parties to their places.
- Introductions
  - Mediators introduce themselves, translator, and/or observers. Ask how each party would like to be addressed. Introduce institution within which mediation is being held.
- Begin with a Review
  - Say that before the mediation begins, it's best to review the mediation process—even if the parties are already familiar with it—just to make sure the process is fresh in everyone's mind. (This language is recommended instead of asking the parties if they are already familiar with mediation. This is to avoid one party saying it's more familiar with the process than the others, beginning the session in a bit of a superior position.)
- Voluntary
  - Note that mediation is voluntary, and thank the parties for taking advantage of the process.
- Self-Determination
  - Note that it's the parties' process, not the mediators'. It's a venue in which parties can:

- Express their concerns
- Seek to understand each other
- Explore their options
- Come to an agreement—if they choose to
  - Even if not coming to a formal agreement, the session may be useful because parties had a chance to listen to one another, talk with one another, and perhaps learn from one another.
- Mediator Role/Collaborative Process
  - Mediators are there to help parties work together. *Together* means that parties should not see sessions as one side striving to win an argument against the other side. It's best to see themselves on the same side, facing a challenge together. Any progress toward meeting that challenge means that all parties benefit (win-win).
  - Impartiality and Confidentiality
  - Mediators are to be impartial between parties and keep confidentiality. No information on the session leaves the room. Mediators' notes are destroyed at the end of the session. Mediators (except on rare occasions) may not be called as witnesses if a court case ensues.
- Exception to Confidentiality
  - In New York State, mediators must report evidence of child abuse.
- Taking Notes
  - Parties are encouraged to take notes, especially if they want to answer something the other side said, but don't interrupt while the other side is speaking.
- Court Admissibility (In New York State Mediation Centers)
  - Except for rare instances, nothing said in mediation sessions is admissible in court, freeing parties to try out all sorts of ideas, with no fear that what they say can be then entered as evidence that they were guilty or wrong about something.
  - Stress that the mediation center is not a court and the proceeding is not a trial. It is not a matter of determining guilt or who's wrong. It's not even a matter of witnesses or evidence.
- Planning Session
  - The mediation session is a planning session for the parties to live together in the future more harmoniously than during the current dispute.
- Caucus
  - At some point, the mediators or the parties may want to have private meetings between each party and the mediators.
  - If this takes place, each party meets with the mediators for the same amount of time, and each meeting is confidential. Only the party itself can allow what is said in a caucus to be disclosed to the other parties.

- Ground Rules
    - The mediators address ground rules for the mediation session, including asking the parties for their suggestions and a request of parties for a commitment to ground rules agreed upon.
    - Examples of ground rules: allow one another to speak and show respect for each other.
- Questions
    - Mediators ask parties if they have any questions about the foregoing.
- Begin
    - Mediation commences. (See following.)

Mechanics of the Mediation Process: The Discussion

Note that the following appears as a neat step-by-step process, but it is only a guide. Human interaction rarely follows neatly prescribed patterns. Mediators must remain flexible. It's better to keep an eye on the goal of a mutually satisfactory outcome. The exact order of the steps to that goal, or even the exact steps to that goal, are not set in stone.

The Situation Described

Each party is asked to describe the situation as he or she sees it and make suggestions for a collaborative resolution. The mediators display active listening and strive for impartiality and self-awareness of their own biases. They attend, probe, clarify, and paraphrase. After each party finishes, the mediator thanks the party who spoke as well as the other parties for listening patiently.

Mediator Reframes

When all parties have spoken, the mediators reframe the presentations, not in terms of stated positions, but in terms of underlying needs, feelings, and values, with special attention to common and complementary ground. If there are many issues, and/or if there is much complexity, the mediators prioritize the issues to be addressed. An issue is a clash of positions or the existence of an unmet need. It almost always involves respect and recognition. Empowerment (and maintaining a balance of power) is also often involved.

Help Parties Understand Each Other

If possible (depending on the emotional atmosphere of the session) see if one can have the parties empathetically describe one another's perspectives, with feedback for confirmation and corrections. If this is not working, or working only partially, the mediators may have to be the ones to reemphasize empathetic understanding among the parties, and highlight the various perspectives in the room. The mediators may also continue aiding in building rapport and trust, working with parties to help vent emotions and minimize misunderstandings.

Reframe and Brainstorm

The mediator sums up again, this time with an eye on the future. This is a good time for the mediators to remind themselves that, if there is to be an agreement, it should come from the parties themselves. Therefore, this is the time for the mediators to encourage brainstorming for collaborative outcomes. Brainstorming is designed to produce as many ideas and options as possible so that parties are open to fresher ways of thinking and moving forward productively. After much brainstorming, with many options on the table, the mediator encourages the parties to choose those options that seem to make the most sense to them and combine them into an integrated agreement, perhaps written out.

Agreement Standards

There are a number of guidelines for effective agreements. Here are the most crucial:

- If there is to be a written text, the agreement stipulations should appear in the text as follows:
  - Party A and Party B agree that:
    - First stipulation.
    - Second stipulation.
    - Etc.
- The agreement should use positive language. No blame should be admitted.
- The responsibilities of the agreement should be balanced.
  - Example: If a party is paying off a debt, the creditor should agree to provide a written acknowledgment of the payment.
  - Example: If the child agrees to do his homework, mom should agree to work with him or her on some of the more difficult exercises.
- The agreement should be doable. One should be able to answer the question, "What if?"
  - Example: If dad agrees to pick up the child from school every Friday at 4:00, how would the parties handle the situation of a traffic jam that will make him late? (Such a stipulation is typical in child custody cases.)

"No Agreement" Is Not Failure: Some Considerations[7]

It is important to point out that, although the goal of an agreement is favorable, also very important in a negotiation or mediation is the development of a new and expanded understanding of the circumstances, perspectives, and needs of each side, even if parties are not able at the time to come to an agreement. Whether the negotiation or mediation is on an interpersonal, community, or international level, the opportunity to develop better relations among parties is of great value. An important aspect of the process is the possibility of transformation (as noted). Transformation asserts the belief that conflict can be a catalyst for deep-rooted, enduring, positive change in individuals, relationships, and the structures of the human community.

Finishing Up

- Have an outside mediator check the agreement.
- Have the parties confirm and sign the agreement.
- Request that the parties keep in touch with the meditators on how things are going.
- Let the parties know that they are always welcome to return to refine/update the agreement, or just to schmooze.
- Thank the parties for choosing mediation and for their hard work.
- And parties should be welcome to return, even if they did not reach an agreement.

"As conflict—difference—is here in the world, as we cannot avoid it, we should, I think, use it. Instead of condemning it, we should set it to work for us. Why not? What does the mechanical engineer do with friction? Of course his chief job is to eliminate friction, but it is true that he also capitalizes friction. [...] The friction between the driving wheel of the locomotive and the track is necessary to haul the train. All polishing is done by friction. The music of the violin we get by friction."[8]

NOTES

1. R.J. Lewicki, D.M. Saunders, B. Barry, J.W. Minton. (2004). *Essentials of Negotiation*. (3rd ed.; New York: McGraw-Hill/Irwin.)

2. J.A. Schellenberg. (1996). *Conflict Resolution: Theory, Research, and Practice*. Albany: SUNY Press.

3. E. Raider, S.W. Coleman, Collaborative Negotiation. New York: Columbia University. Teachers College, ICCCR, 1998 and International Center for Cooperation and Conflict Resolution (ICCCR), Collaborative Conflict Resolution (New York: Columbia University, Teachers College, ICCCR, 2006).

4. R. Fisher, D. Shapiro. (2005.) *Beyond Reason: Using Emotions as You Negotiate*. New York: Viking.

5. Sources: These process descriptions are founded on material presented in the following Teachers College, Columbia University courses: Fundamentals of Cooperation, Conflict Resolution and Mediation, TJ6040, Peter T. Coleman, instructor, Summer B Term, 1999. Basic Practicum in Conflict Resolution: Collaborative Negotiation and Mediation Skills, ICCCR Professional Trainers, Summer B Term, 1999. Advanced Practicum in Conflict Resolution, TJ 6350: Part One, James Williams, Patricia Hunter, instructors, Summer

B Term, 1999. Organizational Internship in Community Mediation, ORLJ5012B 004, Stephen Slate, instructor, fall, 1999.

6.   In addition to the above sources, this introduction was heavily influenced by Krister Lowe, a fellow student in the above-listed courses, currently a senior partner with Ideas for Action LLC and host of the Team Coaching Zone Podcast.

7.   Ronald S. Kraybill, Alice Frazer Evans, Robert A. Evans. *Peace Skills: A Manual for Community Mediators.* (San Francisco: Wiley/Jossey-Bass, 2001).

8.   E. M. Fox and L. Urwick, eds. *Dynamic Administration: The Collected Papers of Mary Parker Follett.* (London: Pitman, 1973).

CHAPTER 19

AN INTRODUCTION TO ARBITRATION AND ADJUDICATION

By Diana D. Juettner and Paul J. Juettner

WHAT IS ARBITRATION?
WHAT IS ADJUDICATION?

AN OVERVIEW

Adjudication and arbitration can be effective means of settling conflicts when other methods have proven ineffective. However, resolution is now up to an independent party, not the conflicting parties, so underlying issues that may be the cause of the conflict might not be resolved.

Adjudication or litigation in a court and arbitration before a decision maker both remove the decision-making power from the parties. Laws and contracts control the decision, not feelings. Underlying grievances that perpetuate conflict are not an issue unless they contravene the law in question.

At the other end of the spectrum is arbitration and adjudication where someone besides the parties makes the decision—the decision of what to discuss as well as what goes into the final decision. No longer can the parties freely express their side of the story or their concerns about how the dispute will be settled.

In other parts of this text, authors have discussed methods for resolving conflict that are in the hands of the parties such as negotiation, mediation, and coercion. In these types of situations, the disputants are active parties to the situation and decide how the conflict can be resolved.

So the game has changed. The parties must now learn new rules and new tactics for managing conflict in these arenas. Since an independent third party is the decision maker, the third party must be made aware of the facts surrounding the conflict. When the parties are in court, only those facts that relate to the law of the case can be considered. In arbitration of a contract, only those facts that relate to the contract can be considered.

Since arbitrators and judges have not lived with the conflict as the parties have, how facts are developed can be important to obtain the solutions we desire.

WHAT IS ARBITRATION?

Arbitration is one form of dispute resolution that engages a third party to resolve disputes. Engaging in the process can be voluntary or mandatory and is usually established by mutual agreement of the parties. An arbitrator can be an attorney or an expert in the subject matter of the dispute. Not all arbitrators are attorneys. The process can call for one arbitrator or three arbitrators to determine the outcome of the dispute.

The arbitrator(s) will listen to the dispute, review the submitted evidence, and then make a decision. The decision may be final, binding, and enforceable, depending on the rules set up by the parties in advance or that have been set forth by contract. A participant has the legal right to be represented by an attorney, to bring witnesses to testify, to cross-examine witnesses, and to present evidence.

WHEN COULD I BE SUBJECT TO ARBITRATION?

Have you ever gone on a cruise? Purchased tickets to a sporting event?

Next time you do so, look at the fine print that accompanies your cruise material or on the back of your ticket to an event. What you will discover is that you cannot take your dispute to court because a clause or section of the contract you agreed to reads that you may only go to arbitration to present your case for a refund once your claim is denied by the event sponsor.

Most agreements that are entered into for goods and/or services include a section that requires the parties to settle their disputes in arbitration. Attorneys for the seller write these agreements; if you wish to buy the product or services, you do not have an option as to whether you would like to use arbitration or go to court. For example, when you want to buy an app for your phone, you will be asked to consent to conditions set forth by the owner of the app by clicking "I agree." If you don't consent to the seller's terms, then you will not be able to purchase their product or service. This isn't a very plausible option because most goods and services require the consumer to agree to this form of dispute resolution. Arbitration is the method of choice by vendors because it is faster, more cost effective, and uses a less formal process in the resolution of a dispute.

WHAT IS ADJUDICATION?

Adjudication is a process in which the court decides how a dispute is to be resolved. This process engages the power of the courts to provide an enforceable conclusion. The courts hear cases that involve a range of disputes from breaches of multi-million-dollar contracts between corporations, liability in automobile accidents, criminal matters, divorce and family matters, and community complaints. Because there are so many cases before the courts, the rules of civil procedure require the parties to make a good faith effort to settle their dispute before it goes to trial. If a case goes to trial and the litigants are not satisfied with the result, the parties can file an appeal to the appellate court to review the case.

WHAT IF I WANT TO TAKE MY CASE TO COURT?

When you as the litigant go to court, you are asking the court to make a decision in the dispute. Litigants must follow rules of procedure and evidence that are complex, structured, and restrictive, and usually require the services of an attorney. Be aware that you will be asked to discuss settlement options as your case goes through the litigation process. When your case gets to trial, you may only bring in evidence relating to the dispute that is acceptable under the rules of procedure and evidence. The judge is not looking at the underlying emotions and issues that have led up to the dispute. The judge will make a decision based on the admissible facts and the applicable law. The decision might not solve the problem at hand because the court will likely not have addressed the underlying issues and feelings.

DOES A COURT ORDER ALWAYS SOLVE A DISPUTE?

Not always, because the order may be difficult to enforce. For example, when neighbors are arguing over the noise level of music coming from another apartment, the court can issue an order to keep the noise level down at a certain time; however, if the neighbors have not agreed to a method of doing so, it is a difficult decision to enforce. The goodwill of the neighbors is needed to make sure that the court order is obeyed. The police can be called to quiet the situation, but they can't be there at all times to see that the decision is enforced. In these instances, Community Mediation Centers can be helpful because they provide feuding neighbors, friends, and family members an opportunity to mediate in a neutral environment. This can be a better form of dispute resolution if the parties are willing to participate.

CHAPTER 20

MEDIATOR ETHICS IN DISPUTE RESOLUTION

By Dr. Stephen E. Slate, Executive Director of IMCR

WHAT IS ETHICS AS IT RELATES TO THE MEDIATORS IN DISPUTE RESOLUTION?

The purpose of this chapter is provide the reader with the chain of events that led to the use of ethical standards at the Institute for Mediation and Conflict Resolution, Inc. (IMCR) as well as similar Community Mediation Centers in the city and state of New York. The relevance and impact that these guidelines had in shaping the roles of mediators and the mediation process as a whole are also addressed. The document reflects a comprehensive view of ethics[1] as it relates to professional mediators in the field of alternative dispute resolution from 1969 to the present.

As we embark on this chronological journey, our Alternative Dispute Resolution (ADR) history centers on the origin of IMCR, which was established in 1969, thanks to the vision of its founding fathers, Theodore Kheel (1914–2010), George Nicolau, Basil Paterson (1926–2014), Lewis B. Kaden, and Arthur H. Barnes. In 1970, a mediation/arbitration training center was established in New York County to train a wide variety of professionals at home and abroad. Following the success of the training center, in 1975, IMCR opened New York City's first community mediation center in Harlem, in response to the socio-cultural unrest of the time triggered by a variety of interpersonal disputes between and among residents in the Bronx as well as New York County. At the time, the Dispute Resolution Center represented a viable, nonthreatening, alternative forum of the people, developed by the people, and for the benefit of the people. It represented a safe forum in which they could address their interpersonal disputes via a hybrid process called Med/Arb. As teaching professionals in the field of arbitration and negotiation at Cornell University, the founders thought that skills used in the hybrid processes would enable community members to address their interpersonal concerns free of cost and hassle, and be less time-consuming than addressing these matters in court.

During the early stage of the Dispute Resolution Center, there were specific procedural guidelines to not only educate the mediator/arbitrators, guide them in their voluntary community roles, and build the trust of potential clients, but also to inform the public of relevant information regarding the nascent process. The ongoing need for training followed and IMCR's eclectic sixty-hour Med/Arb training designed with a focus on a series of goals and objectives, conflict resolution theories, practical role plays, and the Code of Professional Conduct for Mediators,[2] which provided the foundation for the center's high-quality services to the community. These comprehensive codes included the following topics:

- Responsibility of the mediator to the parties
- Responsibility of mediators to the mediation process
- Mediation process
- Appropriateness of mediation
- Mediator's role
- Publicity and advertising
- Neutrality
- Impartiality
- Confidentiality
- Use of information
- Empowerment
- Psychological well-being
- Law
- Settlement
- Termination of mediation
- Responsibility of the mediator toward other mediators
- Responsibility of the mediator toward his or her agency and profession
- Responsibility of the mediator toward the public and other unrepresented parties

In 1981, Judiciary Law Article 21-A, Community Dispute Resolution Centers Program was enacted to address definitions, establishment and administration of centers, application procedures, payment procedures, funding, rules and regulations, and reports. From this point forward, self-determination[3]—one of the salient principles of mediation, which was enjoyed earlier by disputants at the Community Mediation Center since 1975—began a slow process of erosion caused by emerging operating procedures and new ADR guidelines that gradually took away the decision-making power of the center.

The Med/Arb process, which was so beneficial to the courts by reducing its large backlog of mainly frivolous cases, came to an end after the Supreme Court, Bronx County, New York, rendered its decision in the arbitration case *Wright v. Brocket*, May 9, 1991. Very briefly stated, this was a landlord/tenant matter that was addressed at IMCR through the Med/Arb process. The matter was not mediated, but went to arbitration wherein an award was issued in favor of the landlord. The arbitrator's ruling was later introduced in the Supreme Court for enforcement.

After further review by the court, the motion to confirm was denied and the award was vacated on the ground that there was a failure to follow the procedure of CPLR Article 7511[b][1][iv].[4]

Since 1993, following directives of the New York State Dispute Resolution Centers Program, IMCR focused solely on the process of mediation based on the following premise: "Human beings have what it takes to make a difference in their lives. They are capable of transforming themselves, and the environment in which they live." Dr. Thomas Christian, executive director of the state's ADR office, approved the new direction of the organization and certified the center's mediation trainer; IMCR's mediation training has been ongoing ever since at the local and international levels. It established training relationships with local academic institutions such as Columbia University (not ongoing) and Mercy College (since 2000); along with training services to local grassroots organizations and public organizations as well as academic institutions in Central and South America.

After the demise of Med/Arb at IMCR, mediation was viewed in 1998 as, "A private, usually voluntary, discussion and consensual decision-making process in which one or more impartial persons—the mediator(s)—assist people, organizations, and communities in conflict to work toward a variety of goals."[5] The notion of mediators' neutrality was discarded in this nationwide consensus, giving way to philosophical discussions that are ongoing. Special attention followed regarding standard procedures and ethical guidelines so as not to repeat the errors of the past. In this light, the center embraced the Mediators Ethical Standards arrived at by the Society of Professionals in Dispute Resolution (SPIDR), currently known as the Association for Conflict Resolution (ACR); the American Bar Association; and the American Arbitration Association as a standard of conduct for its mediators under the umbrella of the New York State Community Dispute Resolution Centers Program. The following eight standards continue to represent the foundation of New York State mediation process and an ethical framework for its pool of certified mediators.[6] It was promulgated in 2005 by the Office of Alternative Dispute Resolution & Court Improvement Programs.

STANDARD I. SELF-DETERMINATION

Mediators should recognize that self-determination is a basic principle of the mediation process, which supports its voluntary nature, and that the primary responsibility for the resolution of a dispute is that of the parties involved in said dispute, in having the freedom to articulate their points of view and decide for themselves that which is in their best interest, free of coercion, intimidation, and other external pressures. The mediator's role in this regard is that of protecting the voluntary participation of all disputants in ways that assure parties' freedom of choice in their decision-making, avoid all semblance of domination as they facilitate the parties' dialogue, and encourage all parties to make their own decisions.

More often than not, mediators get caught up in the parties' dialogue and feel an urge to give advice that in their view would help parties reach an agreement. They tend to forget that an agreement is not the end of the parties' dispute, and that it does not necessarily resolve the issues addressed at the mediation table. An agreement can actually make a situation worse.

STANDARD II. IMPARTIALITY

This ethical standard implies that mediators remain impartial throughout the mediation process. They should at all times exercise their roles in a non-adversarial manner. Mediators should make all effort to provide a fair process in which parties are given ample time to participate. During this engagement, it is quite possible that mediators will analyze matters being addressed by the parties and feel the effects of their exchange. As human beings, this feeling is viewed as normal; however, mediators should not allow said feeling to disrupt their even-handed approach throughout the session. Impartiality refers to freedom of bias or favoritism either in word or action (body language), avoiding an adversarial role in the process. Should a mediator determine in the course of the process that he or she is unable to assure impartiality by maintaining the integrity of the process, he or she should withdraw.

Mediators should provide dispute-resolution facilitation services only in those disputes in which they can be impartial with respect to all parties as well as the subject matter of the dispute, and be cautious in accepting gifts from a party to a dispute during or after the mediation process, given that it casts doubts on the integrity of the mediation process.

STANDARD III. CONFLICT OF INTEREST

Mediators must make an effort to determine facts that may create a potential conflict of interest in the matter being reviewed for facilitation. They must disclose to the parties any current or past relationship with a party to a dispute or an attorney of any party involved in the mediation session, any and all monetary interest they have with a party that may affect the outcome of the process, membership with one of the parties involved, or any close relationship they have with a party that may impact the process. After disclosure is made, the parties can exercise their self-determination rights to agree or disagree with the mediators' participation in the session.

During or after a mediation session, mediators should not solicit or attempt to procure future professional services, whether or not the parties arrive at a mutually satisfactory outcome in the mediation session. This code of ethics emphasizes the obligation of mediators to maintain transparency. In the event there were justified reasons to believe a conflict of interest violated the integrity of the process, a mediator is obligated to withdraw.

STANDARD IV. COMPETENCE

In order for mediators to be effective, they must have procedural and substantive knowledge regarding the subject matter to be addressed in the mediation process. In this vein they are capable of determining whether or not the parties have informed consent necessary to proceed with their exchange of views leading to an outcome of their choice. Mediators should remove themselves if physically or mentally they are unable to meet the reasonable expectations of the parties.

Mediators should not participate in a mediation session if impaired by drugs, alcohol, medication, or other substance or circumstance. They have a duty to recognize the limits of their ability to engage in assignments they are not prepared to address. Mediators must avoid crossing the mediation line in introducing their knowledge in other professional areas in which they are licensed to provide said services. Regardless of whatever other profession mediators may have, they should respond to the parties only as mediators.

STANDARD V. CONFIDENTIALITY

"Except as otherwise expressly provided in this article, all memoranda, work products, or case files of a mediator are confidential and not subject to disclosure in any judicial or administrative proceeding. Any communication relating to the subject manner of the resolution made during the resolution process by any participant, mediator, or any other person present at the dispute resolution shall be a confidential communication."[7]

Mediation sessions held by certified mediators under the umbrella of the New York State Community Resolution Center are protected by the above confidentiality statute, Article 21-A of the New York State Judiciary Law. Mediators must safeguard the integrity and confidentiality nature of the mediation process by maintaining confidentiality of all information garnered from all participants in the session as well as documents presented by the parties to the mediators.

The confidential nature of the mediation process includes information shared by all parties during a public session as well as information shared in a private session in which mediators meet separately with the parties to a dispute. The information given by one party to the mediator in a private session is not shared with the absent party unless the other party agrees to have said information totally or partially shared.

Currently, the New York State office of ADR programs has identified the allegation of child abuse as the only exception to confidentiality. This opinion should also include elder abuse, and credible imminent bodily harm or death threats directed at parties in a dispute.

Dispute Resolution Centers are responsible for maintaining and protecting parties' records on file for several years, pursuant to contractual agreement with funding sources. Under the confidentiality standard, agreements are not considered confidential information. This allows parties to have these documents reviewed by counsel or others, away from the mediation center, prior to signing and returning the same.

STANDARD VI. QUALITY OF THE PROCESS

Mediators are responsible for conducting quality mediation sessions that are consistent with the Standard of Conduct for Mediators as they engage in matters in which they can satisfy the parties' expectations in terms of their training and experience, allowing the participation of witnesses and attorneys in the sessions, therefore honoring parties' rights to due process, even though mediation is not a fact-finding process to determine truth or innocence.

Mediators should terminate a session, withdraw, or take appropriate additional steps to prevent themselves or other participants from jeopardizing the quality of the mediation session. Termination is deemed appropriate if parties do not understand the process, are impaired because of drug or alcohol use, lack informed consent to cognitively address their concerns, request a reschedule, or end discussions at the mediation table. In addition, mediators should withdraw when faced with procedural or substantive unfairness or conflicts of interest capable of undermining the integrity of the process.

STANDARD VII. ADVERTISING AND SOLICITATION

Mediators are obligated to ensure that all advertising or other marketing approaches on their behalf are accurate and not misleading when addressing their professional qualifications, experience, and services. They should not guarantee results, especially if such guarantee could be viewed as favoring a particular type of disputants or industry over another, nor list names of persons served without the consent of said clients.

STANDARD VIII. RESPONSIBILITY TO THE MEDIATION PROFESSION

Mediators are responsible for enhancing the growth and quality of the mediation process in word and deed, exhibiting at all times the ethical standards of the New York State Community Dispute Resolution and Court Improvement Program, which considers all persons providing mediation under its auspices as a member of the mediation profession.

In accordance with the above standard, mediator professionals should embrace diversity in the mediation field and be open to differing views and perspectives; attend in-service training; participate in ADR workshops; and update themselves with relevant research find-ings in the field, thus enabling themselves to help their colleague mediators and the public at large to better understand and appreciate the benefits of the mediation process. Given the diversity of clients pursuing mediation, cultural awareness is of great importance to all mediators.

THE UNIFORM MEDIATION ACT (UMA)

In 2001, the National Conference of Commissioners on Uniform State Laws (NCCUSL) developed and adopted UMA in February 2002 to address the standard of confidentiality in mediation proceedings. Its major concern was that of keeping mediation communica-tion confidential. For this reason, UMA considers a mediation communication confiden-tial, and if privileged, is not subject to discovery or admission into evidence in a formal proceeding.

The UMA Act addresses only whether mediation communications are discoverable or admissible in legal proceedings. Other than preserving the rights of the parties to agree to confidentiality, it does not provide any rules governing confidentiality, generally speaking. So far, eight states have enacted the Act: Nebraska in May 2003; Illinois shortly thereafter; and New Jersey, Ohio, Iowa, Washington, Indiana, and the District of Columbia followed suit in the last two or so years. Other states have adopted similar bills consistent with their views regarding confidential communication in the mediation process.

Although a subcommittee of the New York State Bar Association's Alternative Dispute Resolution Committee was asked to evaluate whether or not UMA should be adopted in New York, it concluded that New York has its comprehensive mediation statutes and may not be ready for UMA, which was so narrowly drawn.

NEW YORK ADR MEDIATOR ETHICS ADVISORY COMMITTEE (MEAC)

As the mediation field continues to expand its service coverage throughout the Americas and the rest of the world, parties to a wide variety of amenable disputes seek to benefit from the self-determined, confidential, and voluntary nature of the process. In our world of emerging technologies, it will become more and more difficult to assure confidentiality, one of the es-sential elements of a successful mediation. Parties to a dispute should be able to rely on the confidential nature of the mediation process in order to share their stories free of fear that these stories will transcend the walls of the mediation room, especially in virtual environments where breach of security is rampant. As stated recently by attorney mediator Maria Eugenia

Sole, "It takes a special profile of mediator who understands certain characteristics and skills to perform to the best of his work, framed in ethics."[8]

In 2006 as a meaningful support of the Standards of Conduct for CDRC Mediators facing ethical dilemmas in their respective Community Mediation Centers, the New York State Community Dispute Resolution Center established a Mediator Ethics Advisory Committee (MEAC) to respond to mediator inquiries and serve as another resource in the promotion of professional growth and consistency of practice in the field within the framework of the Standard Code of Ethics for mediators.

The committee is made up of thirteen ADR professionals from diverse communities in New York State. Members are responsible for considering inquiries regarding dilemmas in the field of ADR, drafting responses to these dilemmas prior to reviewing, and voting on responses before they become official opinions. These opinions can be viewed at the New York State Community Dispute Resolution Center's website along with its list of professional members.

In conclusion, there is still more to be done regarding the new communication trends brought about by a variety of technical innovations and communication devices capable of challenging the very foundation of the present standards of conduct as they relate to self-determination and confidentiality.

REFERENCES

Civil Practice Law and Rules of the State of New York (1992), Looseleaf Law Publications, Inc.: Flushing, NY.

Court Referral ADR in New York State Final Report of the Chief Judge's NY State ADR Project, May 1, 1996.

Forrest Jr., David C. (1983). IMCR Dispute Resolution Center Mediator's Code of Ethics.

Hoffman, A. David (2009). "Ten Principles of Mediation Ethics."

JAMS Mediator Ethics Guidelines.
  www.jamsadr.com/mediators-ethics

Mediator Ethics Advisory Committee (MEAC)
  http://nycourts.gov/ip/adr/MEAC.shtml

Sole, Maria Eugenia (December 2015). "e-Mediation: A New Stage of Ethics"
  http://www.mediate.com/articles/SoleME4.cfm

Standard of Conduct for NY State Community Dispute Resolution Center Mediators (2004–2005).

Uniform Law Commission
  http://www.uniformlaws.org/ActSummary.aspx?title=Mediation Act

NOTES

1. Principles of conduct governing an individual or a group.

2. Code adopted in the early years by IMCR from the Center for Dispute Resolution in Denver, subjected to future revision.

3. Determination by oneself or itself, without outside influence. Freedom to live as one chooses, or to act or decide without consulting another or others.

4. "Failure to follow the procedure of this article, unless the party applying to vacate the award continued with the arbitration with notice of the defect and without objection." IMCR's submission form used as its Consent to Arbitrate did not unequivocally state that the parties consented to arbitrate and that they were aware that the arbitrator's decision was final and binding.

5. Concept of mediation as introduced by the National Association for Community Mediation (NAFCM) after a national consensus in the winter/spring of 1998.

6. Mediators are certified by Community Mediation Centers throughout the 62 counties. There is no New York State mediation certification.

7. S 849-b Establishment and administration of centers (6), Article 21-A Community Dispute Resolution Centers Program.

8. Mediate.com article published in December 2015.

EPILOGUE

LOUIS

Louis James II, my firstborn son, was a wonderful gift of joy; he was his own person from birth. As his mother, I was able to be the first to embrace him, to cherish him, and to appreciate the miracle of his being. His playful spirit, his passion for life, and his magnanimous love would spread beyond the short 21 years and four days that he lived. On Friday, February 4, 1994, my beautiful son was savagely stabbed to death—in a case of mistaken identity.

With his brutal murder, I realized the lost things that I can never get back are my precious child and the *blessed ignorance* of acute, indescribable grief. However, I've learned that grief is the price one must pay for love. Grief never ends, but we learn to live with the pain and hide the suffering. I see grief as a passage, not a place to stay. It is neither a sign of weakness nor a lack of faith. My students, my colleagues, and the study of conflict management gave me my reason to continue to live and work. My students are *my* Louises.

That a mother can only be as happy as her saddest child means Louis's killer condemned me to a life of depression and sorrow. Well, I was not willing to let that sociopath destroy my future completely. This horrific experience has tinted my lenses. I see the world through the experience of being a homicide survivor. I see my students through the lenses of a parent of a murdered child. My main function in life now is to ensure that every one of my students learns the necessary skills to navigate the dangerous world. I believe Louis did not know enough to trust his instincts when he perceived evil.

My Louis's earthly life spanned only twenty-one years, but his magnificent spirit lives on in each of my students.

After Louis's murder some people would tell me, "I know what you're going through…" or "I know how you feel…" or "the passage of time will make you feel better...." Others tried to explain how I should and would feel. This completely shut me down. I stopped listening to them. I thought those people were so far off, so clueless that engaging them would be a waste of time and energy. They knew nothing about what I was feeling and I wrote them off as emotional illiterates.

I read this Victim's Impact Statement (shown here in part) at court when killer Anthony DiSimone was released with time served (only seven years, three months, and 22 days) for intentionally murdering my son Louis Balancio II. I was not speaking to the killer, or to the attorneys, or to the judge. I was speaking for the public record because I wanted to support the next family who would need to come to court when DiSimone kills again.

Impact statement read on December 10, 2010
New York State Supreme Court, White Plains, New York

My name is Dorothy Balancio. Before February 4, 1994, I would have defined myself as a happy wife, mother, good daughter, sister, aunt, cousin, neighbor, and teacher. My life as a teacher kept me connected to my sons and all their friends. Life was fun and full of blue skies and sunshine. Then, on February 4, 1994, I became a homicide survivor! My life changed from joy to tortured hell! I now am a member of a group called Parents of Murdered Children. For the past 16 years, four or five times a week, I visit the cemetery and talk to an etched picture of Louis on a black granite grave stone. Now there are only dark clouds and storms!

Today I stand before the court as the forever grieving mother of Louis James Balancio. My son was savagely and brutally murdered by sociopath Anthony DiSimone.

As Louis's mother I frequently become emotional when I speak about this heinous crime against my family, this cowardly and savage assault that ended my son's life, permanently damaged all those who knew and loved him, and robbed us all of loving relationships that will never be—never, because that part of our future has been extinguished.

As a mother I will speak about this impact from my heart.

However, I also stand here as what the court might call an expert witness. I have many academic degrees, including several master's degrees, a Ph.D., and multiple postdoctoral certifications from New York State, Cornell University, Columbia University, and Harvard Law School. I was an NYU visiting scholar. My credentials are in the areas of society and group behavior, family and life planning, communication, conflict, mediation, and dispute resolution.

I bring this to your attention because I become passionate whenever I speak of this nightmare.

I don't want you to misinterpret my *passion and pain* for *irrationality*.

Confessed killer Anthony DiSimone is a *sociopath*.

Black's Law Dictionary defines *sociopath* as a depraved killer with no guilt or remorse. Loosely, a mentally ill person who is unstable and can devolve into aggressive, perverted, criminal behavior.

On 9/27/2010, this depraved sociopath swore before you, Judge Adler, that he "stabbed Louis multiple times in order to kill him," casually confessing as if it was to a shoplifting charge.

[I observed that this sociopath pled guilty with cold indifference. Emotionless. His facial expression, body language, and overall tone showed complete apathy—no remorse whatsoever.]

On 2/4/1994, this confessed cowardly assassin attacked an unarmed, innocent 21-year-old.

He didn't know Louis and stabbed him multiple times—what does "multiple times" mean? He stabbed Louis thirteen times in the back.

... it was NOT once or twice or three times,

... not four times ... not five or six or even seven times,

... not eight or nine or ten times ... not eleven, twelve,

BUT THIRTEEN!

This beast executed my beautiful son by stabbing him OVER and OVER and OVER and OVER and OVER and OVER and OVER and OVER and OVER and OVER and OVER and OVER and OVER! According to the death certificate:

- Louis's heart, lung, and kidney were destroyed
- his spine was severed
- there were multiple stab and incised wounds of the back

Cutting into someone's body with a knife is so intimate and personal—so terrifyingly cold-blooded and, keep in mind, he did not know Louis.

What kind of unstable, sick *evil* commits such an act?
(*In my opinion, Anthony DiSimone is criminally insane.*)

To add to this horror, the coroner said Louis survived for 15 minutes to half an hour, lying in the cold street where this sociopath threw him. My poor baby died alone and in agony on that freezing winter night.

What kind of *cruel monster* is capable of such insensitive callousness?

In 10/2000 at DiSimone's trial, there was a PowerPoint presentation of Louis's horrific autopsy. The funeral director told my husband Jeff that in the 25 years of preparing bodies for burial, he never saw such a viciously mutilated corpse. This professional undertaker was visibly upset by the condition of my son's body; in fact, he didn't charge us for some of the funeral expenses.

What kind of unstable, sick heartless fiend is capable of such a heinous act?

[These gruesome images of Louis's butchered body were met with cold indifference by DiSimone—he was emotionless, apathetic. He sat there in the courtroom viewing the results of his horrendous action like he was watching cartoons with his young son.]

In the summer of 2009, unfortunately, I arrived at the courthouse security checkpoint at the same time as sociopath DiSimone and his wife. [Recognizing that I was the mother of his murder victim, he approached me with coldness and indifference—his expression and body language showed no emotion or remorse. His demeanor and lack of eye contact struck me as if he were an individual with no soul. He walked with an arrogant swagger, and his wife screeched across the courthouse lobby that I "should drop dead!"]

Today this court releases this sociopath into the community and history will judge these proceedings. Pollsters estimate that for every letter written by a person to influence a sentencing, there is a minimum of fifty others with similar passion. You, Judge Adler, have 191 letters articulating the need to confine sociopath Anthony DiSimone.

Evil men are not made in an instant—
It takes generations to develop this kind of evil.
This process recognizes that we can no longer just respond (or rush in) to a crisis
and try to save drowning children,
but we must stop those who are throwing the children into the water.
We need to make structural connections and eliminate this element.
We must stop all that feed off this slime.
This is not merely a passing storm,
but a permanent weather pattern.
We need to implement a climate change!

***

On September 11, 2001, thousands of people were killed before our eyes. It seemed beyond comprehension. It was unimaginable that the haven of our societal freedom and democracy were so violently invaded. As a result, we, as a nation, became homicide survivors. It is important to understand that our grief is very different. It is pervasive, profound, long lasting, and cannot be shaken off.

Chronic Stress. A common reaction to traumatic events is not only crisis anxiety, but also lingering stress. Because this stress is with us 24/7, it is harmful physically, psychologically, and spiritually. (My audiologist told me that my hearing loss was probably a result of chronic stress.) In this state of constant stress, we are not always aware of the reason for our depressed feelings. Remember, our feelings are the way we choose to translate the emotions we are experiencing. To further complicate this situation, if someone was already in a state of chronic anxiety (stress from work, relationships, finance, etc.) when the traumatic event occurred, their system often cannot handle the overload in a healthy way. There is very little energy or ability to focus on the new loss and added stress. The predictable world of understandable and expected losses does not help manage this situation. The unexpected death coupled with the violence takes longer to absorb. This means that rituals do not have meaning immediately. The shock delays the ability to mourn.

We are all pained and shaken by the horror and tragedy of the events of September 11, but we can cope optimally in the aftermath of something so frightening, so unpredictable. The goal is not to *get over it*, but rather to work together and *get through it*. I found that people were the language of God for me, because it is very difficult to hear God when your heart is so badly broken. So, I depended upon the people of the criminal justice system.

Louis was not killer DiSimone's only victim—my younger brother, Nicholas, is another. Louis's Uncle Nick died prematurely when his heart stopped on Monday, August 11, 2003. Uncle Wonderful, as Louis referred to Uncle Nick, lived in a constant state of chronic stress after his favorite nephew's murder:

Nick became an active player in searching for the murderer, questioning eye witnesses and following information from the street. He was obsessed.

Nick received death threats from members of a local crime family.

It is useful to maintain an awareness of grief representing a major change in our lives. We need to keep the grief component in perspective as a reminder that we need to act in order to not allow this event to overwhelm us. This can help us adapt and focus on being realistic and appropriately aware of danger in the future. This awareness enables us to control our stress and therefore manage our anger.

Grief has many ways of manifesting. There is not only the loss of a person, but also the loss of security, the enormous increase of vulnerability, and the loss of peace and tranquility that usually are taken for granted. There is no safety and no trust. We need to always be on guard. I realized that grief doesn't just visit for a horrible, temporary stay. It moves into your heart and never leaves. However, grief brings humility and empathy for others in pain as housewarming gifts.

CPSIA information can be obtained
at www.ICGtesting.com
Printed in the USA
LVHW062323281118
598435LV00002B/9/P